P9-DEA-071

"John Beckett's book *Mastering Monday* is a memoir and tutorial on how a young CEO faced down adversity and achieved remarkable success in business along with personal fulfillment by ordering his life and work around the people and principles in the Bible. If you, like me, want to know what the real thing looks like, this is it."

J. STANLEY OAKES JR., PRESIDENT, THE KING'S COLLEGE, NEW YORK CITY

"John Beckett's *Mastering Monday* is a further development of the theme he discussed in his first book, *Loving Monday*. The secret that nurtures the connection between faith and work lies in understanding Beckett's passion to walk intimately with Jesus in his personal life, constantly seeking practical wisdom from the Bible. This book serves as a guide to all kingdom business practitioners."

TETSUNAO YAMAMORI, INTERNATIONAL DIRECTOR, LAUSANNE COMMITTEE FOR WORLD EVANGELIZATION; COEDITOR, *ON KINGDOM BUSINESS*; PRESIDENT EMERITUS, FOOD FOR THE HUNGRY INTERNATIONAL

"This is a fantastic book written by one of America's premier business leaders. John does a masterful job communicating the leadership lessons born of wisdom and faith that mark every successful, competent leader. Every page is lined with fresh insights."

GAYLE D. BEEBE, PRESIDENT, SPRING ARBOR UNIVERSITY

"*Mastering Monday* focuses on the business workplace, but its call to a life of Christian integrity is equally applicable to all professions. Today, when cynicism and narrow self-interest seem to dominate our culture, these personal stories celebrating and illustrating the power of service and the practical value of the Christian walk are truly heartwarming. In simple and gracious style, John Beckett reminds us by modern example and biblical reflection not only that the Christian faith is true but also that Jesus' lordship brings abundant life—even at work."

IAN HUTCHINSON, PROFESSOR AND HEAD OF THE DEPARTMENT OF NUCLEAR SCIENCE AND ENGINEERING, MASSACHUSETTS INSTITUTE OF TECHNOLOGY

"This is yet another powerful book by John Beckett wherein his passion and insight into working with God can help us all produce lives, products and services that represent our Master as well. It comes from a man whose integrity, and what he has actually produced, punctuate it with a quiet, compelling authenticity."

DENNIS PEACOCKE, PRESIDENT, STRATEGIC CHRISTIAN SERVICES

"If *Loving Monday* convinced you that your faith belongs at work as much as it belongs at church, *Mastering Monday* will give you the confidence and the foundation to not only integrate faith and the workplace but do it boldly. Someone needs to make a difference. . . . You are that someone."

PAT WINGEN, FOUNDER AND PRESIDENT, AaLADIN INDUSTRIES INC.

"I have had the privilege of knowing John Beckett for many years. I have visited his company and interacted with his employees. *Mastering Monday* is not theory, but evidence of what God can do through an individual life. This book is an encouragement to any business leaders who want to make a difference where God has placed them."

ANDRÉ THORNTON, AUTHOR, BUSINESSMAN, FORMER FIRST BASEMAN FOR THE CLEVELAND INDIANS

John D. Beckett

Mastering Monday

A GUIDE TO INTEGRATING FAITH AND WORK

IVP Books

An imprint of InterVarsity Press
Downers Grove, Illinois

InterVarsity Press
P.O. Box 1400, Downers Grove, IL 60515-1426
World Wide Web: www.ivpress.com
E-mail: mail@ivpress.com

InterVarsity Press® is the book-publishing division of InterVarsity Christian Fellowship/USA®, a student
movement active on campus at hundreds of universities, colleges and schools of nursing in the United States of
America, and a member movement of the International Fellowship of Evangelical Students. For information
about local and regional activities, write Public Relations Dept., InterVarsity Christian Fellowship/USA, 6400
Schroeder Rd., P.O. Box 7895, Madison, WI 53707-7895, or visit the IVCF website at <www.intervarsity.org>.

All Scripture quotations, unless otherwise indicated, are taken from the Holy Bible, New International
Version®. NIV®. Copyright ©1973, 1978, 1984 by International Bible Society. Used by permission of
Zondervan Publishing House. All rights reserved.

While all stories and examples in this book are true, some names and identifying details have been changed to
protect the privacy of the individuals involved.

Design: Cindy Kiple

Images: Photodisc/Getty Images

ISBN-10: 0-8308-3385-4
ISBN-13: 978-0-8308-3385-6

Printed in the United States of America ∞

Library of Congress Cataloging-in-Publication Data

Beckett, John D.
  Mastering Monday: a guide to integrating faith and work / John D.
Beckett.
      p. cm.
  Includes bibliographical references.
  ISBN-13: 978-0-8308-3385-6 (cloth: alk. paper)
  ISBN-10: 0-8308-3385-4 (cloth: alk. paper)
  1. Work—Religious aspects—Christianity. 2. Employees—Religious
life. 3. Business—Religious aspects—Christianity. I. Title.
    BT738.5.B38 2006
    248.8'8—dc22
                                                                              2006004126

| P | 18 | 17 | 16 | 15 | 14 | 13 | 12 | 11 | 10 | 9 | 8 | 7 | 6 | 5 | 4 | 3 | 2 | 1 |
| Y | 18 | 17 | 16 | 15 | 14 | 13 | 12 | 11 | 10 | 09 | 08 | 07 | 06 | | | | | |

To the Lord, who is always good,

and to Wendy and our family—

now numbering more than twenty—

such visible evidence of his goodness.

Contents

Foreword

We live in a world of either-or dichotomies, and faith and work can seem like polar opposites. But the "sacred" and the "secular" need not be opponents. Instead, each can shed light on the other. In fact, the workplace can become an ideal setting to experience the love of God. The Spirit can transform even trivial matters, engendering faith and bringing fresh joy.

For obvious reasons, the public wants companies to move toward ethical behavior and practice. We have all been hurt by the scandals of unscrupulous business leaders. Our heroes have feet of clay. We are frail human beings who need a relationship with God if we hope to traverse the temptations and trials of this world. We need God's help to become the loving servants we were created to be.

Throughout time, men and women of courage and conviction have given us guidance about our relationship with God and each other. Their lives demonstrate that when we love the Lord our God with all our heart, soul, mind and strength and love our neighbor as ourselves, our individual and collective lives are transformed.

This is why I am grateful for John Beckett's example and the insights in this book, *Mastering Monday*. I have come to know John in recent years and have been inspired by his life and work. At one

conference of corporate CEOs, I saw a twenty-minute video about
how faith and work have been integrated at his company, R. W.
Beckett Corp. I was so impressed with his story that I made arrangements with John to provide a copy for our entire national
board of directors for the Center for FaithWalk, our Lead Like
Jesus ministry. I trust that through this book, many will likewise
benefit from his experience.

But John is a modest man who does not tout his own accom-
plishments; rather, he directs our attention to those who have
been role models and inspirations to him. Principal mentors high-
lighted in this book include biblical "companions on the journey"
who held positions of power and frequently faced situations similar to those in today's workplace. He also tells about modern-day
"heroes" of faith and service and identifies principles that have
guided them. Such lives are inspirational indeed, for we all need
enduring models in whose steps we may follow.

Reading *Mastering Monday* has brought me real joy. It explains
in simple and profound ways how each of us can transform all our
moments, be they at work or play, into God-centered, other-centered
droplets of delight. It helps us get in the groove of our true purpose. It also encourages us to keep listening to the still, small voice
that reminds us that it all begins and ends in service. Enjoy!

Ken Blanchard
Coauthor of *The One Minute Manager*® and *The Secret*

Acknowledgments

The yearlong effort to write *Mastering Monday* was a labor of love, but not isolation. Many helped. I especially want to recognize the editorial assistance of Dick Leggatt, my long-time friend, and Al Hsu, my editor at InterVarsity Press. Special thanks to Pam Madalone, my wonderfully able assistant, and to several fellow business leaders who contributed their stories for this book: John Aden, Dean Borgman, Archie Dunham, Eric Pillmore and David Pugh.

Mike Zigarelli, dean of the Regent University Graduate School of Business, graciously surveyed alumni for contemporary challenges they are facing, and I've addressed several of their questions. My great appreciation to Ken Blanchard—a very busy guy— for the foreword, and to our company's leadership and employees, who manned the ship while I buried myself in this project. And to all—dozens, including Wendy and other family—who reviewed early drafts and made great suggestions. As a friend of mine said, "If you ever see a turtle on a tree stump, you can be sure he didn't get there by himself."

Introduction

In my short lifetime, man has split the atom, conquered polio, walked on the moon and shrunk the globe through the Internet. But millions of us have yet to master Monday.

Monday carries special challenges. For most, Monday is the unwelcome portal from the weekend to the workweek—the creaky door we have to push hard to open, its hinges made rusty by two days of rest.

"Don't buy a car made on Mondays," advise automotive insiders. "Too many assembly plant no-shows; and the ones who do come to work are only half there."

I'm not immune to Monday's challenges. If there's a day in the week when I'm apt to get a headache, it's Monday. Some fare much worse than me. In fact, the Centers for Disease Control in Atlanta cites nine o'clock Monday morning as the peak period for heart attacks!

Yes, Monday is a unique day—the launching pad for the rest of the workweek. But because work itself is often viewed as a "necessary evil"—to put food on the table and fund nonwork passions—poor Monday often gets a bad rap.

For many, however, this negative Monday stereotype is changing—especially for people of faith who, for the first time, are sensing a genuine "call" to the workplace. From that perspective, Monday becomes the anticipated first day of a rewarding, purpose-filled week.

Some years back I wrote a book on this subject called *Loving Monday*. It chronicled my journey from a skeptical, MIT-trained engineer to an enthusiastic follower of Jesus Christ—a journey that continued with the realization that I could find deep fulfillment in my "secular" work, just as I might in any other more direct form of ministry. I told how, with the Bible as a guide, I began integrating my two worlds of faith and work. Gradually, and, I believe, as a direct result of the faith/work connection, I saw the business I was heading prosper and become highly regarded in our industry and community.

Since writing *Loving Monday* I've become increasingly aware of an extensive workplace transformation underway. It's as though God has focused great favor on many who are in business and the professions. This is undoubtedly the explanation for numerous media reports and more than a thousand books that have been published on faith in the workplace. Further, over twelve hundred organizations and networks have formed to encourage the faith-work linkage—most of these within the past ten years.

My window into these phenomena comes through extensive networking of my own—traveling, speaking . . . listening. From that networking, here are some of the questions I hear people asking:

- What is the purpose of business from God's perspective?

- How do I reconcile bottom-line financial goals with the needs of employees?

- How do I advance my career in a world that seems to demand that I compromise my beliefs?

- How do I measure success?

- What does it actually look like when leaders bring the two worlds of work and faith together? Are there conflicts with those who don't buy in?

These are vital questions. I hear them repeatedly—convincing evidence that many want their work to be a true calling that draws forth their full passion and yields deep fulfillment. Such questions also reflect a growing hunger people have to deepen their walk with the Lord and apply scriptural truth on the job. They are seeking out role models and practical examples—people and ideas that can help them with the next steps in their journey. My goal in *Mastering Monday* is to help address that growing hunger. It is to assist those who are called to business to apprehend and apply God's ways in their work each and every day.

A ROADMAP

Let me tell you what's coming in *Mastering Monday*. In part one, "My Personal Journey," I recall some of the struggles I've encountered and how these have brought me new understanding of both my faith and my work.

Then, in part two, "Companions on the Journey," I introduce several biblical characters who are tremendous role models for us as we live out our faith in the workplace. I wish I'd had their example as I navigated through turbulent business challenges earlier in my career.

In part three, "God's Workplace Agenda," I focus on five themes
where biblical truths and business realities intersect. I've found
from over forty years of experience in the workplace that these
practical ideas, will, if embraced, greatly enhance your likelihood
of success at work.

Throughout, I weave in three basic concepts:

- *The importance of developing a warm, personal relationship with
  the Lord.* From that relationship, character is forged, and out
  of godly character, biblical thought can be applied to business situations in a comprehensive and sustained manner.

- *A closer alignment of faith and work.* If we envision these two
  worlds as separate circles, our goal is to see those two circles
  move progressively closer to each other and eventually
  merge into one.

- *The multifaceted expression of God's kingdom in the workplace.*
  Jesus didn't come preaching religion; he came proclaiming
  the kingdom. We want to understand how Jesus' view of the
  kingdom can affect relationships, perspectives and priorities
  in our work.

These are broad, challenging issues. But I trust they are on your
mind, and that exploring them further is exactly where you want
to go next on *your* journey.

HIGHER GROUND

Recently I read in the daily devotional *Streams in the Desert:* "Life
is a steep climb, and it is always encouraging to have those ahead
of us 'call back' and cheerfully summon us to higher ground." "Be-

ing ahead," for me, means only having a few more years and mistakes under my belt, with sufficient battle scars to give me great empathy for those heading up the incline.

The devotional continues, "The mountain climbing of life is serious, but glorious, business; it takes strength and steadiness to reach the summit. And as our view becomes better as we gain altitude, and as we discover things of importance, we should 'call back' our encouragement to others."

I hope to encourage you out of the lessons I've learned: to press on in your relationship with the Lord; to see where he is working in your midst; to grasp the redemptive dimension of the challenges you're facing each day; and to hold out a lively hope that God will see you through, building his kingdom in the process. If I am able to help you "reach higher ground," that will be my greatest reward.

PART ONE

My Personal Journey

1

In and Out of the Furnace

I was born into business. My dad was a talented engineer who decided to begin a manufacturing company in the late 1930s, literally in the basement of our home in Ohio. The business and I were birthed about the same time—so this was indeed a productive period in Dad's life!

Though I was only a youngster, I remember the company's earliest large challenge—survival! World War II had severely restricted the supply of components needed to build our product—oil burners for use in residential and commercial heating. To keep the company going, Dad shifted to a completely different line of business, insulating homes in our area.

I was just six years old, but Dad took me along to "help" the insulating crews who worked out of specially equipped trucks. I can still feel the itch from the glass rock wool we fed into a giant hopper to be pumped out into the walls and ceilings of homes being insulated. No thanks to my help, my father kept his small workforce intact and, after the war, resumed burner production.

Toward the end of high school I wrestled with the choice of where to attend college. I was convinced my decision would be closely linked with what would become my career. For some reason, I was torn between business and going into the ministry. My heart wanted to follow my dad into engineering. Acceptance to Massachusetts Institute of Technology (MIT), the nation's premier engineering school and my first choice for college, would have opened the door to pursue that dream. But part of me was drawn toward ministry—simply because it seemed somehow "more worthy." So I also applied to Kenyon College, a liberal arts school in Ohio that included an Episcopal seminary. I hoped my decision would be settled through the acceptance process.

When the first letter of acceptance arrived from Kenyon, I was mildly pleased—but not overjoyed. But when acceptance came from MIT weeks later (what seemed like an eternity) I practically did cartwheels. If I hadn't grown up a proper Episcopalian, I probably would have. The nod from MIT (and my enthusiastic response to it) seemed clear evidence that I could indeed follow my heart into the sciences and engineering.

Later, toward the end of college, the struggle between marketplace and ministry resurfaced. Should I jump right into an engineering job, or take a stint as a military chaplain? I counseled with Dr. Theodore Parker Ferris, the esteemed rector of Trinity Episcopal Church in Boston, who wisely advised against going into any direct form of ministry unless I knew beyond doubt I was called to do so. Days later, I received a job offer from an aerospace firm—a timely signpost toward my future vocation.

So began an uninterrupted career in business, yet one that ultimately did carry with it a dimension of "ministry." Though my "guidance" during those years was shaped mostly by circumstances, I now recognize that God was indeed steering my choices. Still, he had much more in store for me regarding my spiritual growth.

The first installment toward that growth came through a budding relationship with a very special young lady named Wendy Hunt. We met when I was partway through college. The setting? A small camping supply store in Algonquin Provincial Park in Canada, where Wendy was working a summer job to earn money to attend the University of Toronto. Before long, I met her parents. Much to my surprise, I discovered that both Wendy and her family were people of strong faith—with spiritual depth that was new to me. They spoke of a personal relationship with Christ. How different, I thought, from what I'd experienced to that point.

Impressed as I was with the Hunt family, I found it a struggle to align their wholehearted faith with my more "rational" approach. So I waited, and watched. In reality, spiritual pursuits were not my highest priority.

Wendy and I were married after she finished college, and we settled into life together in northern Ohio. I began work with the Romec Division of Lear, Inc., where I helped design guidance systems for missiles and aircraft. Kirsten, our first child, was born a year later, and life, for the most part, was immensely rewarding. Even so, I sensed a missing element. God still seemed distant, impersonal.

A SURPRISE INVITATION

A year after Kirsten was born, my father approached me with an invitation that surprised me, because he had never even hinted at it before. He wanted me to join him in his small manufacturing business. If I said yes to his offer, it would mean leaving the cutting-edge world of aerospace for the low-tech world of home heating. But the prospect of being able to work with my father really excited me, and that clinched my decision.

Working with Dad was better than I could have ever imagined—he the mentor, I the understudy. For the entire first year he openly shared his knowledge and expertise, and I fully expected to continue learning from him for years to come. But those years never came.

On a chilly morning in February 1965, I received a call from our local police department. Dad, age sixty-seven, had been found slumped over the steering wheel of his car, the victim of an apparent heart attack. From the reported location, I knew he must have been on his way to work. My first response was disbelief. Only hours before, he had seemed so healthy, engaged in his work, attentive to his family. We had so many dreams that were unfulfilled. Yet the crushing reality hit me full force—Dad was now gone. Absent my mentor and closest friend, and only in my mid-twenties, I suddenly felt the overwhelming weight of having to lead the company he had founded and nurtured through its first twenty-eight years.

THE INFERNO

Dad's death was not the only tragedy that struck that year. Just a few months later, an emergency call came to my home in the middle of the night from our village fire department—announcing that the Beckett factory was on fire! I shook off what seemed a "bad dream" to realize it was anything but. The exact words from the caller are deeply etched in my memory:

"Beckett—flames are leaping twenty feet above the building—you'd better get out here!"

When I arrived at the plant, my worst fears were confirmed as ghastly red-orange flames danced grotesquely behind the factory windows and pierced the night sky above the roof. Volunteer firefighters had arrived but were understandably fearful about going into the building, not knowing what volatile or explosive substances might put them at great risk. I assured them I knew how to navigate through the building and they finally agreed to let me lead them into the heart of the inferno.

We fought that fire until dawn. Light from the first rays of sun straining through the smoke-stained windows revealed that not all had been lost. In the days that followed, we rallied our small, twelve-person workforce to an around-the-clock recovery effort and were able to make sufficient repairs to restart production. In fact, by some miracle we didn't miss a single shipment to our customers. To this day I'm not sure how we did that!

The impact of these two events upon me was enormous—like bolts of deadly lightning hitting in close sequence. Up to that time, it seemed I could manage by my own wits. Now, my confidence had been deeply shaken. In spite of wonderful support from Wendy and her family, I wasn't sure where to turn. And God still seemed very far away.

It is often said that coming closer to God requires a "leap of faith," a bold plunge into an unknown realm far beyond our natural capacities or understanding. But my stubborn mind had instructed my reluctant feet to stay firmly planted on safe ground. Months passed without answers. Work challenges continued. I found myself discouraged and confused. All the while it seemed that God was quietly, persistently drawing me to himself.

Small things happened to encourage me: receiving a helpful book from a friend, or hearing a speaker who would answer a key question. Gradually, as I came into my late twenties, the fog began to lift. Bit by bit, pieces of a giant puzzle were falling into place.

OUT OF DARKNESS

Though many unsettled questions lingered, I came to the point where I could no longer sit on the fence. I wanted to be right in my relationship with God, whatever it took. But there seemed to be such a chasm between us. That gap was widened by my own selfishness, damaged relationships with people I'd hurt and the nagging guilt of some bad decisions. With all this baggage, how could I possibly establish a sound relationship with God? Was there such a thing as a fresh start?

Though I didn't fully know what to expect, I asked the Lord to forgive me—to take away the obstacles that separated me from him. His response was immediate. Much as a teacher might wipe the classroom chalkboard clean with one great sweeping motion, the Lord released me from all the accumulated debris from my past. At once, I was aware that a great burden had been lifted from my shoulders. I felt washed, clean.

But that wasn't the end of it. My next step took me still further into unfamiliar territory. For the first time in my life I was able to intentionally let go, surrendering myself to God. I said, in effect: "Lord, I give myself completely to you. I don't want to hold anything back. I want to be yours, and I trust you to receive me just the way I am."

What followed amazed me. I experienced a new kind of peace,

certain that God had accepted me. I hadn't earned it, nor did I deserve it. But as I took that step of faith, it seemed he welcomed me with open arms. For the first time I felt rightly related to him. I was no longer far away. In words I only dimly understood at the time, I realized I had been "born again"—that strange term I thought might apply to others, but not to me. (A few years later, I read a remark by John Wesley, the great reformer and evangelist of the eighteenth century. He said that when he gave his life to God he felt "strangely warmed." That is an apt description of what happened to me.) I felt a closeness to God I'd never experienced—and only dimly imagined might be possible. I had found what had been missing!

As I looked back at events leading up to this moment, I could see a clear pattern. In spite of my obstinacy, God had actually been at work from day one to bring me to himself. He had given me parents who loved me and were wonderful role models. He had guided key decisions, like where I would attend college and what career I would follow. He had enabled me to kindle a precious relationship with Wendy and her family. He had sent friends and mentors just when I most needed them, especially during the months following my father's death, then again, after the fire. His hand had been quietly guiding and providing. Yet he had never imposed nor compelled—only waited patiently for me to see my need. Now, finally, I had responded in ways he had intended all along.

2

Integrating Two Worlds

"Life is hard. God is good. Don't confuse the two."

A FRIEND'S COUNSEL TO ANNE BEILER,
FOUNDER AND FORMER CEO,
AUNTIE ANNE'S PRETZEL FRANCHISE.

My new relationship with the Lord began producing some unexpected changes. The Bible sprang to life, its words packing relevance and punch I'd never before encountered. I grew in my appreciation for Wendy's faith, seeing dimensions I had previously overlooked, such as her meaningful prayer life and deep compassion for those less fortunate. A new circle of friends developed—others with a similar desire for spiritual growth. Yet as excited as I was about my newfound faith, it didn't seem relevant in tangible ways to my work. Each day as I headed into the office, I was painfully aware that I was leaving one world to enter the other. My faith and my work were distinctly separate.

I didn't know anyone else in the work world facing this dilemma. Others who were serious about their faith weren't in business. They were in church-related work. Once again, I was confronted by the old battle between the marketplace and ministry. I wrestled with the issue to the point where I was willing to make a radical switch, even to foreign missions work, if that was what God wanted. Yet I felt that if there were such a thing as a "call" to business, it was to business that I had been called.

In one of my initial bold steps as a young Christian, I "hounded heaven" for clear direction. The answer didn't come immediately, but there was a point when I sensed a tremendous assurance. The Lord seemed to say to me, "John, you're exactly where I want you, serving me in business. This is your calling." I remember the sense of relief and gratitude that welled up inside me—prompting me to make a clear commitment to the Lord in response: I would do all I could to bring my faith to work. I wouldn't be one person on Sunday, and another on Monday. I would avoid "business as usual," with its cut corners and compromise. I would try to lead our company in ways that would honor and please him.

Thus began my journey to integrate two worlds. To my surprise, I found that my growing faith was often relevant to work issues—but the reverse was also true. Workplace issues challenged and strengthened my faith, occasionally more than I'd anticipated.

AN EARLY TEST

I recall an incident involving two employees who had a serious dispute with each other. Earlier, I would have taken a conventional approach to conflict resolution—discussions with each, possibly bringing in outside counseling. But this time, I asked the Lord for guidance, not really sure if or how he would answer. Shortly after, I happened on a Bible passage that says, "If your brother sins against you, go and show him his fault, just between the two of you" (Matthew 18:15).

I determined to take the practical step recommended by this verse: the two would first meet together to work toward resolution. "Don't come out of the room until you've made some real progress," I said. Under that edict, they talked with each other until they found the root of their misunderstanding. Once this surfaced, they were able to ask forgiveness and come out of the room teary but smiling. Their success working this through actually produced a bond that became tighter than ever. Over the years I found this approach to be effective time and time again. In rare cases where it wasn't, we would involve others to help work toward reconciliation.

ONGOING CHALLENGES

With the company growing and adding new people in the early seventies, we were suddenly blindsided by my worst nightmare. A labor union sought to organize our workforce, by then nearly thirty hourly employees. The confrontation is etched in my memory as though it occurred yesterday. Gratefully I can say that our employees voted to retain their nonunion status, and we were able to maintain direct and open relations with all our people rather than going through a third party. But we'd had a wake up call. Unintentionally we had taken our people for granted. We immediately began a process to reshape our practices and policies around a new and much deeper commitment to our people and their well-being. Important lessons! Today, with over six hundred employees, all our companies remain nonunion.

Other challenges landed on our doorstep. Twice in the 1970s our business was shaken by global energy crises. Fuel prices surged upward, riling every market for our products. The impact was so severe that some of our competitors became discouraged and got out of the burner segment of their business altogether. But as with the attempted unionization, these crises had a silver lining. From them we made some changes in our market strategy, developed improved combustion technology and by the mid-1980s had become the market-share leader in our industry. More important, we were learning a new level of determination—and faith— in how to respond to changes outside our control.

Within a few years we began diversifying into some entirely new businesses. Beckett Air, Inc., was founded to manufacture blower wheels for air-moving applications, and Beckett Gas, Inc., to produce gas combustion products. We realized that with multiple facilities and hundreds of employees we needed to establish and communicate standards that would keep us on the same page culturally. We decided to have our managers take a fresh look at our policies and practices. Did they accurately reflect who we wanted to be, encouraging balance between work and family, concern for employee health and safety, the desire for our people to grow as individuals and in their jobs? Could we make these new guidelines live in peoples' hearts, not just their minds? Were they honoring to God in every way possible?

It was more work than I ever expected, but eventually we produced and began communicating our "Corporate Roadmap," which spelled out our vision, mission, core values and governing principles—a framework to help us forge and maintain corporate character and navigate the future direction of our companies. (Our "Corporate Roadmap" can be accessed at www.beckettcorp.com.) I can't tell you how valuable this resource has been in defining and sustaining the business culture in our various companies. (Though we now have multiple companies, in the following pages I will focus primarily on the R. W. Beckett Corporation, our core business.)

A NATIONAL SPOTLIGHT

By the mid-1990s there were hundreds of indications, large and small, that God was at work in our midst. But we sought to keep a low profile as we forged faith-friendly work environments in our companies. And that's exactly why we were so surprised when the request came to profile our efforts on ABC's *World News Tonight with Peter Jennings*.

A year earlier, the Equal Employment Opportunity Commission (EEOC) had issued guidelines that many felt could have a chilling effect on most kinds of religious expression in the workplace. We publicly challenged their position, drawing us into national media attention. This ultimately prompted ABC News to dig deeper into what they saw as a growing interest in America to use the Bible as a guide to business. Because of our involvements with the EEOC, we landed on ABC's radar screen as a subject for their story.

When the network called to say they wanted the R. W. Beckett Corporation to be "Exhibit A," we were more than skeptical. A cynical report was entirely possible and could cause collateral damage. But in spite of our initial misgivings, we concluded that telling our story might help others, and we agreed to go ahead.

The result was a four-minute feature that aired in September 1995. Remarkably it was both accurate and refreshingly free from the bias we feared. Following the broadcast, Peggy Wehmeyer, ABC's correspondent on the story, called me. "John, I just spoke to

New York, and they tell me more people called with positive comments than with any story we've run on the evening news." Hanging up the phone in amazement, I had the immediate sense that the broadcast touched a deep nerve. People across the nation were ready for a different kind of workplace. In my heart I knew it was time for biblically based faith to break out of the confines of the church into the crossroads of commerce.

I had other calls as well—inventors with ideas to sell, people who begged to come to work with us. One call came from a literary agent in New York.

"Beckett," he said in a gruff voice, "I saw that broadcast. You ought to write a book about it!"

His remark caught me off-guard, so I asked him to walk me through what precisely this would involve.

"Write a few chapters," he responded. "I've got connections with lots of publishers."

A few months later I called the agent to say, with a degree of satisfaction, "I've done what you suggested. Where do I send the sample chapters?"

"Don't bother," he said. "I've lost interest. I've gone on to other things."

I remember the very long walk I took afterward—long enough to cool off from his abrupt and deflating pronouncement. With a cooler head I wrote back to him: "I realize you're not interested in this project, but I want to thank you for getting me off the dime. I'm underway with this book and I'm not going to quit."

Two-and-a-half years later, InterVarsity Press published *Loving Monday: Succeeding in Business Without Selling Your Soul*. Its message struck a responsive chord among people eager to bring down the wall separating faith and work. It's humbling and amazing to report that today, through multiple translations, *Loving Monday* is available to most of the people of the world in their own language. (As I write this, a Chinese language edition, published within that country, has just become available in all fifty-three Wal-Mart stores throughout China!)

The response—first to the broadcast, then to the book and related messages I've been able to give in hundreds of settings—has reinforced my growing awareness of what has now emerged as a very significant worldwide movement. For example, imagine my surprise and delight as I visited the spacious home of Jim Lane, a New York investment banker in New Canaan, Connecticut. There, at 7 a.m. on a Friday morning, their shoes neatly parked near the Lanes' back entrance, were 150 men at their weekly gathering—singing robustly, sharing their personal and workplace burdens, and drawing strength from the Lord and each other. From Connecticut to California, from Toronto to Tampa, at prayer breakfasts, seminars, in living rooms and over coffee, men and women are banding together to talk about their faith—and their work.

Os Hillman in his book *Faith@Work* notes the growth of faith-based gatherings in businesses themselves, where Christian affinity groups have formed over the past decade at companies such as Coca-Cola, American Airlines, Intel, Texas Instruments and Sears. No wonder noted author and speaker Dr. Henry Blackaby summed up this remarkable movement this way: "God is marshalling his people in the workplace as never before in history" (Os Hillman, *Faith@Work*, p. xi).

PASSING A CORPORATE TORCH

We continue to operate our growing businesses in ways that are as biblically rooted as possible. Almost daily, workplace challenges keep our faith fresh, reminding us to stay close to the Lord and his purposes and not become complacent. We want to do all we can to preserve and enhance our corporate culture, knowing how easily it can be lost. A top priority is to develop people in our organizations who deeply internalize our mission, our values, and our desire to honor and be pleasing to God. I am pleased to see members of our family embrace these aspects of our culture as they take increasing leadership responsibility in our companies. This is certainly so with Kevin, our oldest son, who has now succeeded me as CEO in our core business. He and I worked for over a decade toward this transition. (For obvious reasons, we're both very grateful to have avoided the traumatic events by which I was thrust into that role!)

My desire is to see all our companies continue to grow and prosper while holding firmly to our distinctive culture (I serve as the board chairman of each). Beyond this focus, I want to help others in business bring faith and work together. The opportunities are almost beyond comprehension. *Fortune* magazine, in a July 2001 cover story, described those involved in workplace transformation as "a mostly unorganized mass of believers—a counterculture bubbling up all over corporate America—who want to bridge the traditional divide between spirituality and work." This new counterculture, now increasingly organized, may already include you and your close colleagues; if not, it can—whether you lead a Fortune 100 company or work in a corner drugstore.

But if you're at all like me, you need lots of help in your business journey. In the next section, we'll discuss some very special people—biblical role models I have affectionately termed "companions on the journey." Their stories have inspired millions. They are the earliest pioneers in workplace ministry. You may be surprised at the clarity their examples bring as you walk out your calling and purpose in the workplace.

PART TWO

Companions on the Journey

3

Our Earliest Companions

FROM ADAM TO BOAZ

Now faith . . . is what the ancients were commended for.

HEBREWS 11:1-2

As I've met with Christians in the workplace over the past several years, I've found a recurring heart cry. They want to know how to practically bring together the two worlds of faith and work. Here are just a few of the questions I've heard people raise: "How do I walk out my beliefs in a secular company?" "How do I deal with coworkers who lack character or integrity, or with a manager who is engaged in unethical business practices?" "How do I reconcile the need to sustain a solid bottom line with efforts to build integrity amongst employees and other stakeholders?"

Kimberly Bean, who heads her own consulting business in Virginia, asked me, "What would you consider to be the ways of the Lord that guide you in making tough business decisions?" What a great question! If we could truly understand "the ways of the Lord," would we not be able to make huge strides in working through the perplexing decisions we face each day?

I've discovered that to know the ways of the Lord we must

learn from the words of the Lord. But that realization came
gradually.

THE BIBLE: DISCOVERING A COMPASS FOR THE WORKPLACE

In my earliest years I regarded the Bible as a collection of stories,
many of which might or might not be true. Mother read me child-
hood accounts of God's creation, Noah's ark and the flood, Moses'
flight from Egypt through the parted waters of the Red Sea, and
young David's bravery as he slew Goliath.

As I grew older, I found little incentive to read the Bible on my
own, at least with any consistency. Oh sure, I'd occasionally dust
it off and halfheartedly scan some pages, only to get stalled out at
the seemingly endless chronologies. (Did it really matter who be-
gat whom?) I regret that I viewed the Bible—as many do today—
as an item to be tucked away on a high shelf, held in reserve like
an emergency flashlight or a shortwave radio, only to be brought
out in times of crisis.

But after I solidified my relationship with Christ, my attitude toward the Scriptures changed. I began to realize its accounts were
more than interesting stories. They were actually a living account
of God's story, his character and his relationship with us. At the suggestion of a seminar speaker, I began the practice of reading from
the Bible each day. What was at first a duty soon became a delight.
As I took this more regular approach to reading and study, I realized the Bible could provide practical advice in workplace-related
issues—one of the most encouraging and helpful discoveries I've
ever made. That reality is what *Mastering Monday* is all about.

Your journey and mine are significant. Each day we have the

option to "paddle our own canoe" or to align our thoughts, priorities and activities with God himself and to allow him to work through us. That is why it is so important to learn from biblical pioneers in the faith. I've found them exactly the kind of mentors, role models and companions we need—folks much like us who faced the challenges and struggles of *their* day.

More than good examples, they are true friends, companions on the journey.

IN THE BEGINNING

In the Bible's collection of sixty-six books, Genesis is first. It is literally "the book of beginnings." Its first few chapters describe the breathtaking process of creation, then the brief period before the Fall. Those days evidence a remarkable partnership between God and his prized creation—the first man and woman. Adam and Eve had boundaries, but within them, tremendous liberty and freedom.

Work took center stage in those early chapters of Genesis. God is portrayed as one who works, creating out of nothingness a breathtaking universe with light, land, water, vegetation, animals and ultimately mankind. Following this effusion of creative energy he completed the world's first performance evaluation: "God saw all that he had made, and it was very good" (Genesis 1:31). God's nature was, and is, to work. This key aspect of his identity stands in stark contrast to other world religions whose god or gods are passive, abstract, and inactive.

In the pattern of his own nature, God then assigned work responsibilities to Adam—to cultivate the land, to name the animal kingdom, to colabor with his wife, have children with her and offer leadership for his family. Unlike the view we often have of work today, Adam and Eve's work was initially a source of pleasure and noble service to God, a reflection of the Father's own creativity and diligence. It should not surprise us, then, that when a person doesn't work as God has intended, he or she languishes.

DEBAKEY'S SECRET

The importance of vocation in a person's life is underscored by the work habits of Michael DeBakey. An article in the *Journal of the American Medical Association* states, "Many consider Michael E. DeBakey to be the greatest surgeon ever." But rather than his surgical achievements, the focus of a *Wall Street Journal* article was DeBakey's secrets of personal health (*The Wall Street Journal*, March 8, 2005).

At the time of the article, DeBakey was chancellor emeritus at Baylor College of Medicine in Houston. This ninety-six-year-old physician maintained an amazingly active life, including writing, research and lecturing around the globe. The *Journal's* writer who visited this legendary physician said, "His personal habits largely parallel what doctors order. He always has been a light eater . . . he walks from place to place . . . chooses stairs over elevators. He is on no medications, doesn't drink and never smoked. His military uniform still fits him perfectly."

Impressive! Yet what struck me most was the next statement. "But here is what Dr. DeBakey sees as the real secret to his longevity: work. He rises at 5 a.m. each morning to write in his study for two hours before driving to the hospital at 7:30 a.m., where he stays until 6 p.m. He returns to his library after dinner for an additional two to three hours of reading or writing before going to bed at midnight. He sleeps only four to five hours a night, as he always has."

With all the emphasis on leisure and our passion to get to the weekends, DeBakey's "secret" will come as a surprise to many. Yet his pattern of energetic work into his nineties is a good reminder that each of us is designed for personal productivity. As my father drilled into me from the time I could first pick up a shovel, "Hard work never hurt anyone!"

A UNIQUE PARTNERSHIP

But work soon lurched radically away from God's original intent. At first, the relationship between God, Adam and Eve, rather than being tedious, was characterized by companionship, warmth, trust, openness and immense satisfaction, and work was an integral part of it (Genesis 2:15). Their partnership was completely free from the tensions, frustrations and ethical lapses that mark and often mar work relationships today. That is, until Adam and Eve trespassed the liberty they'd been given and disobeyed God. At that point, everything drastically changed.

The Fall had unimaginable consequences. I remember well a conversation with a friend about the great difficulties experienced by people throughout the world—pain, heartache, struggle, corruption—sin in its worst consequences. With tears welling up in his eyes my friend observed, "John, I don't think we have any idea how far we fell in the Fall."

One result of humanity's tragic fall was a drastic change in the nature of work. Instead of being the delight God intended, work

in a fallen world became toil: "By the sweat of your brow you will
eat your food" (Genesis 3:19). Later we will see that this debase-
ment of work was not to be a permanent condition. But at the
point of the Fall, literally everything became subject to corruption—including our daily labor.

Still, work and vocations were deemed essential for men and
women. Cain and Abel, Adam and Eve's first children, tilled
the soil and tended flocks. Their offspring were even known by
their vocations—a farmer, a musician, a metal worker (Genesis
4:19-22). Likewise, many who followed in Old Testament accounts were closely tied to the workplace, such as Joseph, who
became the chief administrator for Egypt's king (Genesis
41:41) and Joshua, who had to muster wide-ranging skills as
the Hebrew people came into their inheritance in the Promised
Land. Now we'll look more specifically at some workplace pioneers—Noah and Moses, and two who are less well known,
Bezalel and Boaz.

NOAH: A MODEL OF CHARACTER

Suppose you were faced with the situation Sherron Watkins encountered at Enron. The Houston-based energy colossus had bur-
geoned from a stodgy gas and oil pipeline company to an apparent
Wall Street wonder, vaulting the company, based on revenue, to
seventh largest in the United States. By the summer of 2001, Ms.
Watkins, a finance vice president at Enron, had become deeply sus-
picious of her company's accounting practices. Could this high-
flying company really be a house of cards? What was the right thing
to do? Taking her concerns to senior management could cost her

job. Remaining silent could jeopardize the entire company.

Ms. Watkins, and others facing major ethical dilemmas in the workplace, can draw insights from Noah, our first "companion on the journey." Noah lived during a period of steadily deteriorating standards: "Every inclination of the thoughts of [man's] heart was only evil all the time" (Genesis 6:5). But God chose Noah for a titanic assignment: to build a vessel that would be used to save civilization. He was chosen—note the character qualities—because he "found favor in the eyes of the LORD." He was "a righteous man, blameless among the people of his time, and he walked with God" (6:8-9).

In addition to character, Noah needed an unusual set of skills to handle the challenge God had given him. The naval architect was God himself, and the only path to success was complete obedience: "Noah did everything just as God commanded him" (6:22). The ark he constructed is believed to have had over 100,000 square feet of floor space (the size of twenty regulation basketball courts) and cubic capacity equivalent to more than five hundred modern railroad stock cars!

It is apparent from the example of Noah that God can do incredible things with one person whose heart fully belongs to him. Such an individual is not only able to muster the needed skills but withstand the kind of ridicule Noah faced, endure seemingly endless delay, sacrifice one's personal agenda and "do the right thing." Sherron Watkins, who we'll consider later in greater depth, was that kind of Noah at Enron.

We now jump forward some eight hundred years to consider Moses, a model of leadership.

MOSES: A MODEL OF LEADERSHIP

China is currently undertaking an enormous construction
project—taming the "Mighty Dragon," the Yangtze River that
flows some 3,400 miles from Tibet to the East China Sea. Suppose
you were named the project manager of the Three Rivers Gorge
Dam, the largest project of its kind in history. The dam will stretch
a mile across and rise 575 feet above the Yangtze River. The area
that will be flooded will displace at least 1.2 million people, half
of whom are farmers. Some current residents are so resolute in
their refusal to leave they vow they will drown before relocating.
Do you have a "companion on the journey" in your leadership assignment, one who has tackled such a massive undertaking?

Moses might be just such a companion. Rescued as a baby from
a death edict, raised in a royal Egyptian household, exiled to the
backside of the desert as a shepherd, Moses was eventually called
by God to deliver three million Hebrew people from the yoke of
slavery. In Moses we find a remarkable compendium of sound
business concepts.

Delegation. Once Moses and his followers had passed through
the Red Sea, he faced the overwhelming responsibility of advising
them and settling their disputes. He was a one-man show! Jethro,
Moses' father-in-law, stepped in to save the day. Noticing that
Moses was wearing himself out, Jethro gave him a key to building
an effective management structure: "Select capable men from all
the people—men who fear God, trustworthy men who hate dishonest gain" (Exodus 18:21). Moses took his advice, adding to his
circle "wise and respected men" (Deuteronomy 1:15).

Perhaps no responsibility of a leader is more important than the careful selection of his or her immediate team. Top leaders will find people even more capable than they are themselves in their areas of expertise. Jim Collins, in *Good to Great*, calls this "getting the right people on the bus." "The executives who ignited the transformations from good to great did not first figure out where to drive the bus and then get people to take it there. No, they *first* got the right people on the bus (and the wrong people off the bus) and *then* figured out where to drive it" (Jim Collins, *Good to Great*, p. 41). Once on the bus, effective leaders delegate authority as well as responsibility.

President Ronald Reagan said, "Surround yourself with the best people you can find, delegate authority, and don't interfere as long as the policy you've decided upon is being carried out." Leaders who delegate well build a work atmosphere of trust, respect and productivity—one marked by openness and candor. They and their team insist on knowing the truth, even if it hurts, so they can deal with reality.

An example of poor delegation, at least in the opinion of the company's board, was Carly Fiorina, the ex-chairperson and chief executive of Hewlett-Packard Co. Shortly before her termination in January 2005, a person close to the situation noted, "Ms. Fiorina has tremendous abilities, but she shouldn't be running everything every day" (*The Wall Street Journal*, January 24, 2005).

Skills. Moses brought men and women alongside who were equipped with exceptional skills, people who could rise to the occasion and shoulder large responsibilities. Some had capabilities far beyond natural talent, much as Noah did in his day. One was Bezalel. This choice servant helps us see how God imparts creativity and skills in the arts, trades, design, architecture and engineering. Moses recognized that Bezalel was *chosen* by God (Exodus 31:1-2) and assigned him to oversee construction of the tabernacle in the wilderness, as well as its furnishings. An important assignment? Indeed, for this was to be the place where God's own presence would dwell: "I have filled him with the Spirit of God, with skill, ability and knowledge in all kinds of crafts—to make artistic designs for work in gold, silver and bronze, to cut and set stones, to work in wood, and to engage in all kinds of craftsmanship" (Exodus 31:3-5). What employer wouldn't want people with Bezalel's skills in their organization? And those skills extended beyond his craftsmanship ability to his capacity to mobilize and train others.

Building a team. Bezalel didn't build the tabernacle by himself. The Lord appointed a right-hand man, Oholiab, to help him. In addition, he developed a team of other skilled craftsmen. "And he has given both him and Oholiab . . . the ability to teach others. He has filled *them* with skill to do all kinds of work as . . . master craftsmen and designers" (Exodus 35:34-35). It is good to note that while God gave these craftsmen skills, they still needed training. We likewise do well to recognize where God has gifted a person, but must also be intentional in helping them build on their God-given gifts.

While Bezalel took personal responsibility to build the Ark of the Covenant (37:1), which would house the tablets of stone with the Ten Commandments, others constructed a gold overlaid table, the atonement cover, the cherubim and lampstand, hammered of pure gold. They made curtains of finely twisted linen and yarn, the acacia wood altar, bronze pots and utensils, the priest's garments of gold, yarn and fine linen, and the breastplate with its exquisite stones (Exodus 25—28). What a wide range of skills were required!

No doubt these craftsmen not only brought a variety of skills to their work but also a variety of temperaments. Whether a sports team, a military unit or a marching band, building a good team involves bringing together people with different skills and temperaments to work toward a common goal. This variety is an asset, not a liability, as long as the team functions with mutual respect and a desire to learn from and support one another.

Tyco International, with 250,000 employees worldwide, is now trying to rebuild after the terribly failed period during which former CEO Dennis Kozlowski led the company to near ruin. Eric Pillmore, one of the new team members who heads corporate governance, told a recent CEO gathering that as with most failed companies, Tyco's previous leadership team was comprised of "yes men" who moved in unquestioning lockstep to the company's CEO. This pattern, he said, has led to some of the most egregious, greed-driven corruption in the history of American business. In radical contrast, Pillmore says, "Today's team members at Tyco are expected to be open and candid in their communications with each other and are evaluated, in part, on this aspect of their performance. Our new leadership appreciates how a diversity of giftings on a well-functioning team can help solve complex problems and accomplish lofty goals." Working together, Tyco's new team is well on the way to turning this huge company around. To the benefit of their employees, creditors and the communities in which they are located, they have avoided the ultimate fate of Enron, which effectively shuttered its doors with the loss of many thousands of jobs.

Cultural continuity. Moses didn't take cultural continuity for granted. He knew how easily the distinctive culture of the Hebrew people could be lost, so he both modeled and taught high standards: "Fix these words of mine in your hearts and minds . . . teach them to your children . . . carefully observe all these commands . . . to love the LORD your God, to walk in his ways and to hold fast to him" (Deuteronomy 11:18-19, 22). At stake were the character and reputation of families and tribes and ultimately even the survival of the entire Hebrew nation.

Achieving "cultural continuity"—getting everyone on the same page—has been one of our business's primary challenges as we've grown. At one time we could assume people we hired would come to us with basic character qualities such as honesty, punctuality and good work habits. We no longer can make that assumption. Often the societal forces that influence personal qualities are diametrically opposed to our values-based environment. So our company's leadership has made a major commitment to teaching and training as a means of transmitting our expectations and standards and sustaining our corporate culture—a primary purpose of our Corporate Roadmap, mentioned earlier.

Tyco has done a superb job of recasting and transmitting a values-based approach as they've guided their organization through massive organizational and cultural change. They've developed a "passport" that clearly spells out the ethical standards by which the company will be guided, and they've made it a top priority with their leadership throughout the world to align the thinking and conduct of each employee with the new guidelines. Pillmore says, "It's a huge challenge, but unbelievably rewarding when people actually adjust their behaviors around the company's high expectations and standards."

Succession. Most of us don't think about our successors. But in organizations of every size, succession is a primary concern for leaders. In fact, the renowned management consultant Peter Drucker said succession is the last great challenge of management. In the final chapter of his life, Moses thought much about his successor. He understood the stakes: the nation's destiny depended on the right choice. He had groomed a younger man named Joshua, and when the time was right, Moses commissioned him: "Now Joshua son of Nun was filled with the spirit of wisdom because Moses had laid his hands on him" (Deuteronomy 34:9). The book of the Bible named for him, Joshua, attests that he was an outstanding successor to Moses. Joshua took the reins of the nation and, for the first time in over four hundred years, they entered their Promised Land.

Ideally, planning for succession needs to begin well in advance of the transition. The history of many businesses, large and small, is that succession is often handled poorly. When the wrong person is set in place, it can radically demoralize the workforce and even imperil the company. Surprisingly often the short-term fix is to bring the former leader "out of retirement" to stabilize the business until a proper successor can be found. Succession also fails when it is postponed too long, perhaps by a leader who is reluctant to give up the reins and clings to the position. This, too, can demoralize younger potential leaders.

Succession that is done well will not only preserve the best of the organization's attributes but also set the stage for the kind of progress that fresh thinking and fresh energy can bring. I see this happening in our company under its new leadership as our son Kevin forges a new team and undertakes fresh avenues for growth, all the while holding tenaciously to the values we both believe are so important.

We can learn from Moses' "model" handoff to Joshua that a godly approach to succession can be very rewarding, but it requires earnest prayer, attentiveness to where God is working, mentoring, careful planning and good timing.

BOAZ: A MODEL OF CARING

Imagine you've decided to sell your family business and have begun the search for a new owner/CEO. Of course he'll need good leadership skills, but you especially want a "people person," someone who can relate well to employees, suppliers and others. Is there a biblical companion who personifies the kind of leader you need to put in place?

Meet Boaz. Hidden away in the book of Ruth, Boaz is introduced as a wealthy property owner and "a man of standing" in his community. As he arrives at his farm he greets his harvesters. And what a greeting! "The LORD be with you!" he calls out. "The LORD bless you!" they reply (Ruth 2:4). Can we not picture Boaz with a winsome smile? Can't we sense his wholehearted appreciation for his workers—and theirs for him?

I enjoy visiting manufacturing plants. My hosts are generally eager to point out the production equipment, the systems and processes, and the facilities themselves. I'm always glad when I see that these important elements are in good shape. But my primary interest is in the people. Are they valued? Is there rapport with them? As we wend our way down aisles and around machines, I notice whether there is eye contact with the people, an indicator of whether they are recognized and appreciated. Often there isn't, causing me to wonder if they're viewed almost as incidental. How people are treated is one of the most important benchmarks of effective leadership and a subtle but reliable indicator of true success in business. People throughout an organization want to know they're truly valued, and if they are they will contribute in extraordinary ways.

By contrast with some leaders in today's work world, Boaz was different. He was warm, courteous, compassionate—one who "has not stopped showing his kindness to the living and the dead" (Ruth 2:20). How becoming for this unusual leader, and what a fine companion on our journey. If I were looking for a future business leader, I'd love to find someone with the people skills Boaz possessed.

Not Unlike Us

Actually, Noah, Moses, Bezalel and Boaz were not so different from you and me. Initially they spent years of their lives in seemingly unspectacular work assignments—tending sheep, growing crops, engaged in various trades. But they were "in school"; they were learning to manage people, work through difficulties, overcome doubts and fears. They made mistakes. But what uniquely qualified them to move into positions of increased trust and influence was more than talent. Each had developed a deep and abiding bond with God, and this is the unique challenge for each of us who is called to the workplace.

As we saw, Noah "found favor in the eyes of the LORD" (Genesis 6:8). Moses was in awe of God: "Who is like you—majestic in holiness, awesome in glory, working wonders?" (Exodus 15:11). Boaz and Ruth were esteemed by God and were granted the honor to became the grandparents of David, placing them directly in the line from which the Savior came (Ruth 4:17). Indeed, it was *faith* they were commended for (Hebrews 11:1-2).

Here is the great encouragement we should draw from their lives. For each of us to succeed as Christians in business will take more than a bundle of skills. It will take more than reliable character, diligence in our work, capacity for leadership and organizational abilities, as important as these are. Success ultimately requires a steadfast resolve to faithfully serve and please God.

The workplace pioneers we've considered thus far help us know that this is entirely possible—we can cultivate hearts for God, learn what pleases him and maintain the confidence that he will guide us in exactly the paths he has chosen. Who knows what "exploits" he has in mind for each of us!

4

Biblical Wisdom for Today

DAVID AND SOLOMON

If we learn to worship God in the trying circumstances,

he will alter them in two seconds when he chooses.

OSWALD CHAMBERS

David Pugh faced a dilemma. As the head of a $1.6 billion New York Stock Exchange-traded distributor of industrial products, his challenge was this: he and his company's top management were on totally different pages regarding corporate pricing strategy. And with that realization came a growing sense of urgency to get this discrepancy rectified.

For several weeks, his senior managers had been meeting with major suppliers. With drumbeat regularity these suppliers had warned that their prices would be going up. This would put a serious squeeze on the company's earnings—just at a time when they were seeing sustained financial improvement for the first time in years. The issue was whether these increases could be passed on. The company's customers had come to expect price decreases, not increases.

David's concern was that his normal communication with his

managers had failed to energize them sufficiently for the tough action that was necessary. How would he break the logjam that seemed to loom larger with each passing day? Even he was surprised when direction came the way it did.

In David's daily reading of Proverbs at the breakfast table over a cup of coffee, the words of verse 20:4 seemed to leap off the page: "A sluggard does not plow in season; so at harvest time he looks but finds nothing." As he thought about it, he realized this verse about the direct relationship between plowing and harvest applied specifically to his dilemma. So while still at the table, he wrote a memo to his top managers quoting this passage. It was titled "As for Price Increases—'To the Plow!'" (David kindly gave me permission to excerpt from his memo.)

> What great imagery perfected in so few words! Much is written about the sluggard, none of it good. It brought to mind our position today in preparing to pass on to the market the price increases that we are receiving and are going to receive. Are we plowing now? If not, the harvest will be bare.
>
> We are not seeking to unfairly take advantage of anyone or of any situation. In the past, in a misconstrued effort to be kinder and gentler, we have failed to push price increases when the time was right. As a result, we fell behind our competitors in achieving fair margins. We must not allow this to happen again.
>
> We have worked too hard, have come too far, to bear the pain of backsliding at this point. For all of us, *now* is the season to plow. No bare harvest for this team!

The company moved ahead with fresh conviction, the necessary pricing adjustments took effect, and margins were maintained. As of this writing, the market value of David's company has increased by over 40 percent since they took that bold action. Wisdom from the book of Proverbs, written thousands of years earlier, had been God's way of directing a large company's CEO and his managers.

In this chapter we will look at two "CEOs"—actually kings in their day—who had to face some of the same issues we encounter in our places of work. The two are David and his son Solomon. Both were among the most influential leaders who ever lived. Five books of the Bible tell us much about their history —1 and 2 Samuel; 1 Kings; and 1 and 2 Chronicles. In addition we read many of their reflections in Psalms, Proverbs, Ecclesiastes and Song of Songs (or Song of Solomon). David and Solomon's influence is still evident centuries later.

DAVID: CALLED TO BE KING

Our first encounter with David is as a young lad whom the prophet Samuel has chosen in preference to his seven older brothers to be Israel's next king. Though he seemed the least likely, he was clearly the Lord's choice. Samuel had to be reminded that God calls people for specific assignments, but not according to the criteria we often use: "The LORD does not look at the things man looks at. Man looks at the outward appearance, but the LORD looks at the heart" (1 Samuel 16:7). This isn't bad advice for us as we think about hiring criteria!

J. Lee Gwaltney, a marketing manager in Virginia, recently

asked me, "Does God 'call' people to a specific career, profession or company?" Most of us would agree that God may call people to ministry or church work, but we are less certain when it comes to other vocations. That God, through the prophet, sought David out to become the king of Israel should encourage Mr. Gwaltney and each of us. Without a doubt God calls people not only into spiritual pursuits but also to political leadership, as with David, and to every other work arena that is worthy. As a friend of mine says, you can be an "ordained plumber!"

Even in his youth, God had worked in David to forge the character qualities he would later need. When Samuel found David, he had already demonstrated bravery as a warrior and skill as a musician. At various times these actually became his professions— "callings" at certain points in his life. By age thirty, the young shepherd, musician, poet and warrior had become king.

A Heart After God

Even as a powerful monarch, he remained determined to walk closely with God: "Then King David went in and sat before the Lord" (2 Samuel 7:18). This wasn't so much an incident as it was a lifestyle. I cannot but wonder whether David's absolute devotion to the Lord transcends his many giftings and enormous talent and is the main reason for his success as Israel's greatest king.

David's deep yearning for an intimate and enduring bond with his Father is most evident in the psalms. To David that relationship was primary—far beyond merely understanding and applying principles. A few examples:

- Create in me a pure heart, O God, and renew a steadfast spirit within me. (Psalm 51:10)

- I desire to do your will, O my God; your law is within my heart. (Psalm 40:8)

- I seek you with all my heart . . . I have hidden your word in my heart that I might not sin against you. (Psalm 119:10-11)

- I love you, O LORD, my strength. (Psalm 18:1)

- I trust in your unfailing love. (Psalm 13:5)

- My heart is set on keeping your decrees to the very end. (Psalm 119:112)

David, above all else, had a heart after God.

A DISASTROUS DETOUR

Sadly, this man who loved the Lord with such passion also made some very costly mistakes—the kinds that often plague modern executives. In one tragic moment of weakness he fell into an adulterous relationship with Bathsheba, the wife of one of his military commanders (2 Samuel 11). The incident occurred when David uncharacteristically stayed back in his palace when others went out to war. Very simply, he was in the wrong place—making it impossible to do what he should have been doing and possible to do what he shouldn't have been doing. This is in itself a lesson. We must be sure we are at *our* post, taking seriously our responsibilities.

David's lust for Bathsheba then launched him into a complex scheme to have her husband killed. God was so displeased with these transgressions that he sent the prophet Nathan to rebuke the king. Recounting all God had done to bless David, Nathan said poignantly, "And if all this had been too little, I would have given you even more. Why did you despise the word of the LORD by doing what is evil in his eyes?" (2 Samuel 12:8-9).

There were consequences. There always are. The first child born to David and Bathsheba died, and as the prophet Nathan predicted, calamity haunted David's household for the rest of his life.

What can we learn from David's transgression? First, we have to appreciate the transparent honesty of Scripture. If I were the historian, I might have discreetly deleted this chapter in David's life. After all, he had achieved so much; should this dirty laundry be aired? But the account is provided for a purpose. The failures of others are an example and warning to us (see 1 Corinthians 10:1-13). Indeed, the lesson from David's tragic error reminds me that regardless of how much I achieve, if I become careless, those successes can be obliterated by moral failure.

One of my principal life goals is to "finish strong." I don't take achieving this as a "given," knowing I am very capable of yielding to temptation. I was sobered some years ago by a statement of Billy Graham's that he would rather be taken home by the Lord than be unfaithful to Ruth, his wife. Later I heard Bill Bright, founder of Campus Crusade for Christ, echo the same sentiment regarding his pledge to his wife, Vonette. I've made their commitment my own and have declared it to Wendy. I see it as a significant safeguard, helping protect me from myself, I trust for the balance of my days.

Another lesson from this period in David's life is that in the midst of God's harsh dealings, we also see his grace—extended when David came to God in deep repentance. David was as forthright in his confession as he was deceitful in his sin: "I have sinned against the LORD" (2 Samuel 12:13). "For I know my transgressions. . . . Against you, you only, have I sinned" (Psalm 51:3-4). Just as God forgave David, we should be encouraged that no matter how grievous our sin, our heavenly Father loves us, hears us and forgives us when we ask.

Centuries later, the apostle Paul set a redemptive capstone on David's life: "For when David had served God's purpose in his own generation, he fell asleep" (Acts 13:36). How good to know that in spite of his transgressions, David's legacy is that *he served God's purposes*. I wouldn't mind having that epitaph on *my* gravestone!

SOLOMON: WISDOM FOR TODAY

David and Bathsheba had a second son, whom they named Solomon. (Note this *tangible* evidence of God's forgiveness toward David.) Solomon succeeded David as king. From Solomon came some of the Bible's clearest and most specific insights concerning work, economics, trade, interpersonal relationships and practical wisdom. I once heard a conference speaker say, "If you want to know how to run your business, get a Bible and read the book of Proverbs!" I've found that to be sound advice in my work career.

Solomon's wisdom came as the result of a direct request to God: "So give your servant a discerning heart to govern your people and to distinguish between right and wrong" (1 Kings 3:9). God granted that request, and he grants it today, as we saw in the example of David Pugh. As James in the New Testament instructs, "If any of you lacks wisdom, he should ask God, who gives generously to all" (James 1:5). God is the source of all wisdom.

PROVERBIAL WISDOM

While David inspires me because of his incredible relationship with the Lord, Solomon influences my business life by the enduring wisdom he has communicated through the book of Proverbs. Here are some samples worthy of pause for reflection, words to write "on the tablet of your heart" (Proverbs 3:3).

> Trust in the LORD with all your heart,
> And lean not on your own understanding;
> In all your ways acknowledge Him,
> And He shall direct your paths. (3:5-6 NKJV)

> The LORD will be your confidence. (3:26)

> Blessed is the man who listens to me,
>> watching daily at my doors,
>> waiting at my doorway.
> For whoever finds me finds life
>> and receives favor from the LORD. (8:34-35)

> The man of integrity walks securely. (10:9)

> He who walks with the wise grows wise. (13:20)

> In a multitude of counselors there is safety. (24:6 NKJV)

> A man's heart plans his way,
> But the LORD directs his steps. (16:9 NKJV)

> Buy the truth and do not sell it;
> get wisdom, discipline and understanding. (23:23)

These are powerful ideas—life-altering concepts that stand in stark contrast to the "wisdom of the world." Let's just take Proverbs 3:26 as an example: "The LORD will be your confidence."

Think of all the ways people try to bolster confidence in themselves and others, from pep talks to pills to purchases. What they really need is the Lord. He doesn't just give us confidence. He *is* our confidence.

Prayer for wisdom can be our most important prayer in the workplace. Most of us contend every day with challenges that defy "conventional wisdom." We need a different kind of wisdom, that which comes from above, and remarkably God delights in giving such wisdom. Often—though probably not often enough—I have lifted a puzzling situation to the Lord, asking for his wisdom, and have been surprised to receive a fresh thought or a different perspective on the matter.

THE CUSTOMER COMPETITOR

A practical example of receiving fresh wisdom from above occurred in our business some years ago. Because our company manufactures a highly engineered product, our technology, though only minimally protected by patents, is important to our success. So it was very disconcerting when we learned, quite by accident, that our product had been copied by one of our largest customers. They had every intention of becoming our competitor. Believe me, we asked for wisdom!

There was no obvious way to deal with the situation. Would lowering our price to this customer solve the problem? Not really. The gap between our price and their cost was too large. Furthermore, out of fairness, any price adjustment would need to be extended to our other customers. We pondered other options, but to no avail. Though we were thoroughly frustrated, we quickly concluded that *how* we handled ourselves was paramount. We would take the high road. We would stay professional. We would even do all we could to salvage a customer relationship we had spent decades building.

Weeks passed, during which we lifted up many prayers for wisdom. Then one day, sitting in the living room of a friend in the south of England during an early morning "quiet time," a passage of Scripture quite unexpectedly came to mind. It was a word spoken by Moses to the exiles from Egypt as they faced the formidable Red Sea: "Stand still, and see the salvation of the LORD" (Exodus 14:13 NKJV). Though the solution was no closer in view, this verse gave me my first inkling of hope that the Lord was somehow going to "part the waters." The question was whether I could "stand still" long enough to see it happen.

We had scheduled a meeting with our customer's top executives to reach a final conclusion on how to proceed. Though we had wrestled with this dilemma for months, we had no specific plan— only a reassuring nine-word verse from the Bible. It wasn't until the afternoon before the meeting that a possible solution emerged, actually during a conversation I was having with our oldest son, Kevin, as the two of us were concluding a lengthy automobile trip. But doubts lingered. If the fledgling idea were indeed an answer to prayer, would our determined customer agree to it? A few of our execs got together that evening to pray, committing this whole matter to the Lord.

The next morning the room was tense as we sat down with our customer.

After the usual small talk, they asked, "Well, what do you suggest?"

I really don't know what they expected our response to be. We seemed to be completely boxed in. I took a deep breath. "Here is what we are prepared to do," I said. "We will buy your development—design costs, tooling, everything—and here is our offer price."

They sat in stunned silence. "Are you serious?" they finally asked.

"Dead serious," I replied. "Furthermore we will require a long-term supply arrangement with a noncompete clause."

After a pause, they said, "Please let us meet in private."

Twenty minutes later they asked to reconvene. The next words spoken would chart our course for several years. If they said "no" to our offer, we would soon have to scale back production and reduce our workforce. Furthermore, if they were actually successful producing and marketing their own product, other customers of ours could follow suit, threatening our business even further.

Back in the room together, they simply said, "We accept your offer."

I stayed calm on the outside. But inwardly I shouted *Amen!* as a rush of energy coursed from the top of my head to the tips of my toes. We recommitted to our relationship, secured the product they had developed and continued as a supplier, hardly missing a beat.

The Lord had given us a word of wisdom, first to wait, to not be anxious, but trust in him, and then to follow a specific strategy: "Buy their development." That strategy came at "11:59." It often does. What a reminder this was to me to depend on him, to seek him for the wisdom we need—in small details as well as the large decisions.

How Did Solomon Finish?

One note of caution before we leave Solomon: God had blessed him as fully as any person who had ever lived. In fact, when the Queen of Sheba came to visit him and saw all the Lord had done, she exclaimed: "Indeed, not even half was told me; in wisdom and wealth you have far exceeded the report I heard" (1 Kings 10:7). Solomon's fame extended to the borders of the then known world: "The whole world sought audience" with him (1 Kings 10:24). But wisdom, wealth and fame gave Solomon no guarantee against stumbling. Nor do they for us.

As with so many great leaders, Solomon ran headlong into a defining "however" in his life. "King Solomon, *however*, loved many foreign women" (1 Kings 11:1, italics added). And with the foreign women came their foreign gods. That was a clear offense to the Lord—Solomon's violation of the first commandment: "You shall have no other gods before me" (Exodus 20:3). God had been very direct with Solomon on this matter: "You must not intermarry with them, because they will surely turn your hearts after their gods" (1 Kings 11:2). Tragically that is exactly what happened: "As Solomon grew old, his wives turned his heart after other gods, and his heart was not fully devoted to the LORD his God, as the heart of David his father had been" (11:4). The consequence was disastrous for Solomon but, from God's view, necessary: "I will most certainly tear the kingdom away from you and give it to one of your subordinates" (11:11).

Here is a sobering contemporary reality: the achievements of many outstanding business leaders—people who started strong and accomplished much—have been severely compromised in their latter years. Even as I write this, the board of directors of Boeing unanimously asked for the resignation of their sixty-eight-year-old CEO, abruptly ending his illustrious career in the aircraft industry. His dismissal was not because he wasn't providing good leadership but because of an inappropriate relationship with one of the company's female executives. Ironically, this CEO had come into the job as a champion of corporate ethics, and under his reforms the company was beginning to emerge from earlier embarrassing scandals.

It defies explanation and all logic. A person's guard is lowered. Maybe it's too much idle time or too much discretionary money. It could be the flush of invincibility that often comes with success. It may be spiritual laziness—disregard for the strong caution "that we do not drift away" (Hebrews 2:1). Rather, we are admonished to "hold firmly till the end the confidence we had at first" (Hebrews 3:14). An excerpt from *Streams in the Desert* commenting on this verse says: "The greatest challenge in receiving great things from God is holding on for the *last half hour*." One can't plan for that last half hour. But I believe the Lord's intent is that we live in such a way that the last half hour carries the same nobility as any other point in our lives.

God would want the latter years of our lives to be exceedingly fruitful—a time of influence and opportunity, years when we synthesize the wisdom gained from a lifetime of experience, years when we can impart strength to emerging generations, years when we can wisely steward resources that have been entrusted to us. In a way, these years are a test of all we truly believe. The Lord wants us to succeed to the last. He wants us to finish strong.

We can learn much from these two "CEOs," David and Solomon—from their successes and failures and from the towering legacy of their inspired writings. These are indeed marvelous companions for us on our journeys, providing God's perspective for how we should think and how we should live.

5

World-Class Leaders

DANIEL AND NEHEMIAH

God is continually preparing his heroes, and when

the opportunity is right, he puts them into position in an instant.

He works so fast, the world wonders where they came from.

A. B. SIMPSON

Speaking out carries a risk. But there are times when a person of conviction must not remain silent. To do so carries an even greater risk—violation of that person's integrity. Bill faced such a choice. His story vividly illustrates how a person who is *not* the chief executive can still have profound influence in his or her sphere of responsibility, and beyond.

As division manager of a Fortune 500 company, Bill was deeply concerned about the anticipated succession plans for the company's top leadership position. The man who was the heir apparent had been carefully groomed to be the next CEO but had failed to gain the respect of several senior people in the company, including Bill. Even so, the change seemed inevitable.

After much soul-searching and prayer, Bill decided he had to take his concerns to the current CEO, a forceful and at times volatile leader. He must have felt as Esther did when she petitioned the king: "I will go to the king. . . . And if I perish, I perish" (Esther 4:16). After becoming queen, Esther had learned of a plot to kill all her fellow Jews. She was challenged to take bold action by her Uncle Mordecai with the memorable words: "And who knows but that you have come to royal position for such a time as this?" (Esther 4:14). Intervene she did, with the dramatic result that the entire Jewish population under the king's rule from India to Ethiopia was spared.

To Bill's relief, the meeting with his company's CEO went remarkably well. All Bill's years of effective service, coming up through the ranks in the organization, had garnered the admiration of his boss. Now the seed had been planted that the proposed new leader might not be the right person to take the company into the future.

But the issue was far from settled. It would take more analysis, more meetings—some confrontational and most requiring Bill's direct involvement—and ultimately board action. At the next board meeting a vote was taken, resulting in a vote of "no confidence" in the proposed leader. Bill, with great courage, grace and tact, had quietly guided his company through the most critical decision it would make as it moved into the twenty-first century. In the end, another leader was appointed, a person who brought the right balance of competence, knowledge of the company *and* rapport with others. In the years since the decision, he has proved to be the ideal new CEO.

YOU'RE NOT THE CEO?

As I meet with people in the workplace, I am often asked how believers should function when they are *not* in the top position, especially when those to whom they report don't share their beliefs or even their values. Bill is a great example of such a person, and it is worth examining what enabled him to be the person God used to influence the future of his company.

First, he had earned respect in his sphere of responsibility. In fact, his work unit had become the most sought-after place of employment within the entire organization. Second, he cared for the whole company, not just his own bailiwick. When a major situation arose, he had the courage and character to speak the truth, even at personal risk. Third, he approached this difficult assignment prayerfully and respectfully.

Do the Scriptures give insight into the ways a person like Bill who works for others can be effective? Absolutely. In this chapter we will look at two great examples, Daniel and Nehemiah. Both worked for powerful kings who understood little of their God. Both excelled in the opportunities they had been given—they were faithful in the "small things." Both took great risks, knowing their ultimate accountability was to God, not man. Both changed the course of history by resourcefully navigating through the unique challenges confronting them. Both provide us with practical insights we can apply in our work situations.

DANIEL: SERVANT TO KINGS

Daniel had been brought to Babylon as a young man with other captives from Judah during the reign of the Babylonian king Nebuchadnezzar. Early in Daniel's captivity it became evident that God had significant plans for him and was carefully guiding his formation as a leader. Some examples: "God had caused the official [in charge of Daniel and his companions] to show favor and sympathy to Daniel" (Daniel 1:9). "God gave [Daniel] knowledge and understanding of all kinds of literature and learning" (1:17). When King Nebuchadnezzar had a troubling dream and his counselors were unable to interpret it, God gave Daniel the interpretation (chapter 2).

After explaining the king's dream, Daniel was propelled into one leadership position after another. He served as the modern-day equivalent of adviser, policy analyst and foreign minister, not just in one administration but in three. Under the reign of King Darius, Daniel was made one of a triad of principal administrators. It is said of him that he "so distinguished himself . . . by his exceptional qualities that the king planned to set him over the whole kingdom" (6:3). His rivals became jealous and conspired to have Daniel thrown into the lion's den. But even there, God was with him: "My God sent his angel, and he shut the mouths of the lions" (6:22).

I love the evidence of God's initiative in Daniel's life, indicated by the powerful verbs in the Scriptures cited above. God "caused." God "gave." God "sent." God was clearly active with him, providing and showing favor. Other Scriptures help us understand some of the reasons why.

First, Daniel had become a person of exemplary character, such that even his adversaries could not find flaws: "They could find no corruption in him, because he was trustworthy and neither corrupt nor negligent" (6:4). Second, he had developed a serious prayer life: "Three times a day he got down on his knees and prayed, giving thanks to his God" (6:10).

Daniel's success hinged not on any one factor but on the powerful convergence of these three: his basic character, his prayerful dependence on God and God's initiative. These so defined Daniel's life that even the king credited Daniel as one who continually served God (see Daniel 6:16).

This confluence of character, prayer and God's initiative can shape our lives and influence our success as well. Character is a quality we establish by the choices we make. Prayer is a discipline that grows through use. God initiates where he finds the other two active, just as he did with Daniel.

Are you in a difficult situation? Begin with a character check. Are you knowingly doing anything to displease God? If so, be ruthless with yourself in getting it straight. Have you committed the matter to prayer? Prayer was so important to Daniel that he put his life at risk to keep praying, even against the king's edict. If you have done your part in these two critical areas—personal character and prayer—you can look expectantly for God to intervene, regardless of the circumstance or situation.

This is what Bill discovered when he didn't know where to turn. His solid character qualified him to be God's choice to confront the prickly succession issue in his company. He prayed through every stage of the development, and enlisted the prayers of others. And God took up his cause in an extraordinary way. He will for you as well.

You and I may never be in a role as unique as Daniel's—serving at the highest level in multiple administrations of powerful empires. But his story can inspire us that wherever the Lord places us, we can serve him faithfully and effectively. It's as though God is saying, "You do your part, and I'll do mine."

MORE THAN A CUPBEARER

As with Daniel, Nehemiah gives us much to learn and apply, especially his capacity to take bold action, manage complex projects and relationships, achieve strategic goals, and build a loyal following. Lessons from Nehemiah are as relevant today as they were twenty-five hundred years ago.

Nehemiah's "secular" job in the palace of King Artaxerxes was low profile but required complete trustworthiness. As cupbearer, he had ultimate responsibility to safeguard what the king ate and drank, for the risk of adversaries poisoning the king was ever present. A modern counterpart to Nehemiah would be the chief security guard for a head of state—one who would always have access, one who could be fully trusted, one who at a moment's notice would be prepared to lay down his life for the leader.

Nehemiah was faithfully going about his business when he received the disturbing report that his beloved Jerusalem was in great distress. His courageous, calculated response has inspired many over the years and can serve as a model for us as well. Note these elements: his immediate impulse to pray, his foresight to plan, and his steady persistence as he implemented his plan.

Upon receiving the news, Nehemiah's immediate response was to humble himself before the Lord: "I mourned and fasted and prayed before the God of heaven" (Nehemiah 1:4). The focus of his prayer was not himself or the situation of his people but rather the awesomeness of God. "O LORD, God of heaven, the great and awesome God, who keeps his covenant of love with those who love him and obey his commands" (Nehemiah 1:5).

He then acknowledged his own waywardness, and that of others: "I confess the sins *we* Israelites, including myself . . . have committed against you" (1:6, italics added). He was not above the problem but saw himself as part of it. (I find it refreshing when today's business leaders step up and take responsibility for a problem instead of shifting blame to others.)

Then Nehemiah passionately rendered his petition: "Give your servant success today by granting him favor in the presence of this man [the king]" (1:11). He knew his success depended on God's mercy and favor, not his own position or ability—a good reminder for us that when we fully cast our burdens on the Lord he will hear and help us (Psalm 55:22).

"Gems" from Nehemiah's Action Plan

When the opportunity was right (timing is *so* important), Nehemiah petitioned the king. When the king fired a pointed question at him, Nehemiah lifted an "SOS" prayer to God: "Then I prayed to the God of heaven, and I answered the king" (Nehemiah 2:4-5). Later the apostle Paul would coin the phrase "pray without ceasing" (1 Thessalonians 5:17 NKJV). That's what Nehemiah was doing as he met with the king—a tested pattern for us that the next time we're in the midst of a conversation or meeting, the Lord can be right there with us, only a prayer away.

Nehemiah then asked to be personally involved in rebuilding Jerusalem's walls: "If it pleases the king . . . let him send me" (Nehemiah 2:5). Isn't this one of the hallmarks of great leadership—being directly engaged? (Remember David's decision to stay back from the battle and the ensuing illicit relationship with Bathsheba?) Next came Nehemiah's thoughtful preparation, evident when the king asked how long it would take and what he would need to accomplish his mission. Nehemiah had planned ahead and was able to state exactly what he would require by way of support. (Do you have an important meeting coming up? Thinking through the purpose and agenda in advance will nearly always produce more effective results.)

That same desire for thorough preparation prompted Nehemiah to survey Jerusalem's sad state of disrepair by night (see Nehemiah 2:11-15). I was intrigued to learn that the God-fearing general Robert E. Lee had similar motivation. He insisted on doing his own reconnaissance during the Civil War, riding by horseback into enemy territory to discern firsthand what his army could anticipate (H. W. Crocker, *Robert E. Lee on Leadership*, p. 135). In the same way, a modern executive benefits greatly as he or she gets face to face with customers or employees. I have found there is no better way to be sure we are dealing with reality.

I recall a time when Nehemiah's approach to his mission subtly guided my efforts to "rebuild the walls" in our region of northern Ohio. I had been asked to head up "Lorain County 2020," a community-based coalition formed to address some systemic problems that were hindering growth in our area. Though I'd grown up in Lorain County, I felt I lacked a broad perspective. So as a first step I hired a small plane and a pilot and spent several hours flying over our county to get the large view of its primary cities, major industries, farming, river systems and the shoreline on Lake Erie. Then I visited our cities and towns, looking at the infrastructure, talking to people, and assessing our county's assets and liabilities. We assembled a group of results-oriented leaders and, over the next several years, worked to implement a broad array of fundamental changes in our needy region. I am grateful for the "template" for community action left by Nehemiah thousands of years ago.

BUT NOT WITHOUT OPPOSITION

Nehemiah's effort to rebuild Jerusalem's walls met with immediate opposition from those who mocked and ridiculed, seeking to intimidate and demoralize the workers: "'What is this you are doing?' they asked, 'Are you rebelling against the king?'" (2:19). Opposition is a reality all of us, but especially those in leadership, must face in the workplace. Any good work will be opposed—sometimes from the outside, sometimes from within, occasionally from both directions. While being sensitive to the concerns of others, and without being willfully stubborn, leaders need to be resolute, standing against hindrances that would wear us out and distract us from our mission.

Aware that the incessant barrage from detractors was affecting the people, Nehemiah moved boldly to provide needed perspective: "Don't be afraid of them. Remember the Lord, who is great and awesome, and fight for your brothers, your sons and your daughters, your wives and your homes" (4:14). At times, our posture must be militant. The imagery of how they worked is powerful: "Those who carried materials did their work with one hand and held a weapon in the other" (4:17).

AVOIDING THE TRAP

In spite of the cautionary measures taken by Nehemiah and the workmen, the opposition continued, but with new tactics. This time his detractors sought to draw Nehemiah into a trap: "Come, let us meet together in one of the villages on the plain of Ono" (6:2). But Nehemiah knew their plan was to harm him. His resolute response might well be ours as we respond to that which distracts us from our mission: "I'm doing a great work; I can't come down" (6:3 *The Message*).

If what you and I are doing is God's will, it qualifies as a "great work," whether it is cooking dinner for the kids or designing a bridge to span the Amazon River. We need Nehemiah's resolute response to the many forms of opposition we face, including procrastination, distraction or discouragement. To succeed, we cannot "come down" to all those annoyances that move us off target.

The rebuilding project was completed in a mere fifty-two days. When the final stone was set in place a remarkable reaction occurred: "When all our enemies heard about this, all the surrounding nations were afraid and lost their self-confidence, because they realized that this work had been done with the help of our God" (6:16). What a powerful lesson! When we stand firm, our confidence rooted firmly in God, there comes a point where our self-confident adversaries back off, and victory is at hand.

Among scriptural mentors who integrate faith and work, Nehemiah is without peer. He was submissive to both his God and his employer. He was spiritually mature, wise, focused, determined and effective. He inspired his "ordinary" followers to extraordinary results. We are all honored to have such a companion on our journey.

THE WAYS OF THE LORD

Our visit with Old Testament companions began in chapter three with the question "What would you consider to be the ways of the Lord that guide you in making tough business decisions?" I trust some of those ways have become evident from the biblical leaders we've considered.

- Noah, who stood strong against his critics, obeyed God's bold plan, and was instrumental in preserving both the human race and the animal kingdom

- Moses, who skillfully employed timeless management principles to lead three million people from bondage to freedom

- Bezalel, who constructed God's tabernacle with Spirit-endowed gifts of artistry and craftsmanship

- Boaz, who stood out as a prominent but warm-hearted leader who cared deeply for people

- David, who was passionately devoted to the Lord as a musician, warrior, poet and king

- Solomon, whose practical wisdom still informs our everyday decisions

- Daniel, whose "secular" work for several kings was, in fact, full-time service to the Lord

- Nehemiah, who humbly, prayerfully and with great determination rebuilt a city's walls and revitalized a disheartened people

These and many I've not noted excelled in a work context. They were spiritual statesmen whose examples foreshadow the workplace demands of today's builders, craftsmen, leaders, "kings" and king's servants. Though seemingly larger than life, they were very human. They lived out the ways of the Lord, valuing obedience to God over acceptance by men. They sacrificed for great causes, counting their service to the Lord more important than fame or fortune. They were, as described by the writer to the Hebrews, those "of whom the world was not worthy" (Hebrews 11:38 NKJV).

They also inspired our forebears in the New Testament—men and women who pioneered the most profound "revolution" in the course of history and, as we will see, were themselves deeply immersed in business and commerce.

6

A New Covenant

JESUS AND HIS FOLLOWERS

For this God is our God for ever and ever;

he will be our guide even to the end.

PSALM 48:14

Perhaps you were spellbound, as I was , if you viewed Mel Gibson's *The Passion of the Christ*. Billy Graham said of the portrayal, "I doubt if there has ever been a more graphic and moving presentation of Jesus' death and resurrection."

One scene, a flashback to Jesus' years as a carpenter, provided a lighthearted and welcome pause from the weighty depiction of the last twelve hours of the Lord's life. In the sun-drenched yard just outside the family home, Jesus and his mother had this dialogue:

Mary: Jesus, Jesus . . . are you hungry?

Jesus: Yes, I am.

Mary steps out to survey Jesus' latest project.

Mary: This is certainly a tall table! Who is it for?

Jesus: A rich man.

Mary: Does he like to eat standing up?

Jesus: No, he prefers to eat like . . . so.

Jesus puts his elbows on the table and bends down.

Jesus: Tall table, tall chairs!

Mary glances around, but doesn't see the chairs.

Jesus: Well, I haven't made them yet.

Jesus gives a hearty laugh.

Mary: This will never catch on!

Ever a mother, Mary signals to her son that the meal is ready.

Mary: Oh, no you don't! Take off that dirty apron before
         you come in. And wash your hands!

*Mary pours water on Jesus' hands, and he returns the favor by
playfully splashing water on Mary, then kisses her on the cheek.*

Jesus, the carpenter. Insights into this period of Jesus' life and
the resulting influence on his followers add immeasurably to our
understanding of the Bible's view of vocations and the workplace.
We'll explore these shortly. But first, let us consider some important concepts that bridge the Old and New Testaments.

The New Testament is both a continuation of and a departure
from the Old. It is a continuation because the same God is central
through the transition from Old to New. This continuity is reinforced by a psalm quoted in the New Testament book of Hebrews:
"You remain the same, and your years will never end" (Psalm
102:27; Hebrews 1:12). God's character, his standards of right and
wrong, and his ultimate purposes are unchanging.

On the other hand, the New is a departure. What was *projected*
in the Old is *fulfilled* in the New. In Jesus' words, "Do not think that

I have come to abolish the Law or the Prophets [i.e., the Old Testament]; I have not come to abolish them but to fulfill them" (Matthew 5:17). An analogy by the early eighteenth-century English minister and Bible commentator Matthew Henry helps convey this idea of fulfillment: "If we consider the law as a vessel that had some water in it before, he did not come to pour out the water, but to fill the vessel up to the brim."

Fulfilling the Law and Prophets was but one dimension of the seismic change that occurred in the coming of Jesus Christ. The book of Hebrews emphasizes his *supremacy*. Christ is superior to the angels, for they worship him (1:4-6). He is worthy of greater honor than Moses, for he created him (3:3). He fulfills a need the Aaronic priesthood was not able to, for his sacrifice was once for all time (7:27). His ministry is superior to that of the law, for he mediates a better covenant (8:6).

Oswald Chambers provides this insight into the uniqueness of Jesus:

> Jesus Christ was born *into* this world, not from it. He did not evolve out of history; he came into history from the outside. Jesus is not the best human being, he is a Being Who cannot be accounted for by the human race at all. He is not man becoming God, but God Incarnate, God coming into human flesh, coming into it from the outside. (*My Utmost for His Highest*, December 25)

Jesus' radical invasion into human history set the stage for a new proximity between God and every person. He used distinctive terminology to convey the profound change when he spoke of "the kingdom of God." Let us look at this concept in closer detail, for it has a direct bearing on what the Lord expects of us in the New Covenant.

THE KINGDOM OF GOD

Jesus' initial words in the Gospel of Mark announce his priority: "'The time has come,' he said, 'the kingdom of God is near'" (Mark 1:15). On another occasion he said, "I must preach the good news of the kingdom of God . . . because that is why I was sent" (Luke 4:43). He instructed his followers to make his priority theirs. In matters of everyday life their first responsibility was to seek that kingdom: "But seek first his kingdom and his righteousness, and all these things [material concerns, work, vocations, even such details as food and clothing] will be given to you as well" (Matthew 6:33).

What is the kingdom of God? My close friend Gary Bergel is the president of Intercessors for America and has given some good thought to this question. I like the simplicity of his definition: "The kingdom of God = the reach of God." In other words, God, through Christ, is reaching into every sphere of life with his measureless love, grace, influence and authority.

Writer and editor Al Hsu, in an excellent article titled "A Company? No, More Like a Kingdom," puts an interesting twist on our work as it relates to God's kingdom:

> I often think about what it means that Jesus is king. He declared that the kingdom of God is at hand. As Christians, we are the king's servants. And as in medieval days, every king needs kingdom workers. Some are knights who protect the subjects. Others are artisans, craftsmen and merchants. Some till the land. Others heal the sick. Some educate and

raise the young. Some herald the king's news. Every role is significant if a kingdom is to function effectively and the king is to rule justly. No kingdom runs by itself. (www.TheHigh-Calling.org)

I find this imagery very helpful, though admittedly there are aspects of medieval kingdoms we would be just as pleased to leave behind. However, the King and the kingdom that Jesus spoke of are realities. The real issue is how we relate to these realities.

THE BRIDGE: OLD TO NEW

To more fully bridge between the Old, the New and the kingdom of God, let us look at the remarkable progression from God's *original* intent, found in the book of Genesis, to the *fulfillment* of that intent, revealed in the New Testament.

- *Intimate relationship.* God created men and women to have an open, trusting and intimate relationship with himself—one in which they would walk in obedience and enthusiastic service to their Creator. Work was a joy, an integral part of that relationship—in reality the "kingdom of God" as it first appeared.

- *Violated trust.* Adam violated the trust he had been given, piercing God's heart. That rebellion required God to radically alter the relationship: "So the LORD God banished him from the Garden," setting cherubim to guard the way back (Genesis 3:23-24). But God never lost sight of his original desire for a properly functioning kingdom. In fact, he countered the rebellion with a plan of redemption: "But when the time had fully come, God sent his Son" (Galatians 4:4).

- *Redemption.* Jesus, God's son, left his royal estate with the Father, taking on human form as an obedient servant. (See Philippians 2:6-8.) He actually embodied many of the characteristics of the first man, "Adam, who was a pattern of the one to come" (Romans 5:14). Jesus lived a perfect life, overcoming the temptation to sin that proved fatal for the first man. His ultimate sacrifice on the cross opened, once again, the possibility of a restored relationship with the Father: "For if, by the trespass of the one man, death reigned through that one man, how much more will those who receive God's abundant provision of grace and of the gift of righteousness reign in life through the one man, Jesus Christ" (Romans 5:17).

- *Restoration.* During his days on earth, Jesus revealed the true nature of his heavenly Father. For all who are willing to see and hear, he opened a window into what God's kingdom is like, providing in himself a visible model for how we should think, how we should act, and how we should "follow in his steps" (1 Peter 2:21). By his powerful example he captivated and energized his followers with his compassion, his concern for the small details of their lives and the ocean-depths of his love.

- *Modern application.* Many, even in our own day, have received the redemption the Lord so graciously offers. They have been reborn spiritually, becoming "new creations" (2 Corinthians 5:17). They have apprehended at least a measure of the kingdom of God, here and now, including their work. To me, it is a growing and amazing realization that my redemption intersects with what I am doing day to day as I work in close cooperation with my King.

(A more complete description of personal redemption and transformation is available at <www.LifesGreatestQuestion.com>.)

Now let us glean from a few New Testament "companions on the journey." As with their predecessors in the Old Testament, their lives and examples can inform us as we seek to "master Monday" in our places of work.

JESUS AND THE WORKERS AT HIS SIDE

No scriptural example of workplace mastery is more inspiring than what we find in Jesus' life. Historian Kenneth Scott Latourette has observed, "As the centuries pass, the evidence is accumulating that, measured by his effect on history, Jesus is the most influential life ever lived on this planet. This influence appears to be mounting" (in Josh McDowell, *More Than a Carpenter*). We long for the day when that influence reaches into every thought, every decision and every dimension of the daily conduct of those who seek to follow him.

While I find every facet of Jesus' life and legacy compelling, and as my devotion to him as my Lord deepens by the day, he retains a special place in my heart for his years "in business." A large charcoal drawing hangs over my desk at my office as a good reminder. A powerful rendering of Jesus the carpenter by artist Frances Hook, it portrays Jesus with his muscular arm running a box plane down a piece of wood, his gaze intent on what he is making, his whole character reflecting the excellence of his trade.

For over a decade, Jesus ran a small woodworking shop. Just as we do in our larger business, he had to plan ahead, purchase materials, maintain his tools and inventory, manage the work of others, tend to product quality, please his customers, and pay taxes. He was making real products—tables and chairs, cabinets, oxen yokes for farming. He was meeting real needs.

Can you imagine the immense satisfaction Jesus found in his work, laboring not just to please himself but his Father in heaven? Through his excellence at his trade he was not just learning and practicing valuable skills for use in the future. He was actively modeling and extending the kingdom of God right where he was, amid wood chips and sawdust, rising to the challenges and receiving the rewards of his daily activities.

Jesus' experience as a businessman was foundational for his ultimate call: to be the Savior of mankind. The lessons he learned and relationships he forged as a tradesman influenced the ways in which he brought transformational change to the needy world around him.

- Once Jesus began his active ministry he promptly formed his close circle of disciples. He related with ease to those in the workplace, which perhaps influenced his choice of the Twelve, for all had backgrounds in the marketplace of his day.

- His own reservoir of experiences likely dictated the context for his teachings—parables relating to sowers, merchants, fishermen, and tax collectors.

- As he ministered to and taught others, it was not only in houses of worship, as one might expect, but out where folks were—in the streets, on hillsides, in the intersections of commerce (often to the consternation of the religious leaders who deemed their "religion" to be above such common life).

The influence of the marketplace permeated Jesus' teaching. If references to the trades, business and commerce were stripped away, it would leave a mere skeleton of all he came to influence and change.

Jesus' purpose as he emerged from a work context was to reach the entire world, and this would become the exact mission of his followers. This focus is clear from his final prayer for his disciples. Addressing the Father, he prayed, "As you sent me into the world, I have sent them into the world" (John 17:18). He was commissioning his followers as special agents representing God's kingdom, sending them into hostile territory. Though they would face fierce opposition, the testimony is that they indeed "turned the world upside down" in the spread of the gospel.

The disciples' commissioning to "go into all the world" was not limited to Jesus' immediate hearers, for he continued his prayer, saying: "My prayer is not for them alone. I pray also for those who will believe in me through their message" (John 17:20). If you and I are followers of Jesus Christ, that prayer was prayed for us. I am in awe whenever I think that God's own Son, the carpenter from Galilee, is not only sending us but is right here with us, a companion on our journeys, wherever God places us.

THREE WORKPLACE EMISSARIES

I conclude this chapter by discussing three "workplace emissaries" from varied vocations. Each, out of the context of his or her "secular" work, contributed in extraordinary ways to the growth of the early church. We find them in the Acts of the Apostles, portrayed by a physician-turned-writer named Luke.

By way of introduction, the initial followers of Christ generally accepted that the message of the gospel was to go to fellow Jews. Less obvious was that it was also to go to the Gentiles, who were often deemed outside God's plan for redemption. After all, if the Jews were "the chosen people," didn't that automatically exclude the non-Jews? But God's intent was otherwise, dramatically revealed in a dream to the apostle Peter in Acts 10. God challenged him in no uncertain terms to reassess his deeply held views and consider God's plan of salvation for Jew and Gentile alike.

CORNELIUS

First is the story of Cornelius, the person Peter was led by the Spirit to visit after his dream. As a centurion, Cornelius was an unlikely candidate for the gospel. In the Roman military, a centurion rose to a position of command by being "as tough as nails." But as we saw earlier with David, God "looks at the heart," far deeper than external trappings.

Cornelius's heart was quite remarkable. "He and all his family were devout and God-fearing; he gave generously to those in need and prayed to God regularly" (Acts 10:2). Cornelius's servants, in summoning Peter to come to their master's house, spoke of him as "a righteous and God-fearing man, who is respected by all the Jewish people" (Acts 10:22).

When Peter arrived he spoke to a large gathering of the centurion's relatives and close friends. To Peter's amazement, the "Holy Spirit came on all who heard the message" (Acts 10:44). Later Peter reported the outcome to a council of leaders in Jerusalem. While initially skeptical, they concluded, "So then, God has granted even the Gentiles repentance unto life" (Acts 11:18). Thus Cornelius, a military leader with a heart for God, became the person God used to open the door for the gospel to the Gentiles.

Are you or a member of your family or a close friend in the military? May the lesson of Cornelius encourage you that right there in training camp, while at a military academy or in combat with a mortal enemy, God sees your availability. He can work in you and through you in small and large ways to extend his kingdom.

THE QUEEN'S TREASURER

A second example is a civil servant, an official in charge of the treasury of Candace, queen of the Ethiopians. We don't know his name, only his vocation. Philip, a deacon in the early church, had been summoned by the Holy Spirit to travel to a road leading toward Gaza. There he met the Ethiopian, who had been to Jerusalem on a pilgrimage and was now on his way home.

Philip was able to clarify a passage from the Old Testament that the queen's servant was reading, telling him "the good news about Jesus" (Acts 8:35). The Ethiopian responded wholeheartedly, professing his newfound faith: "I believe that Jesus Christ is the Son of God" (Acts 8:37 NKJV). I can imagine his conversion experience was the highlight of his "treasurer's report," with the account perhaps working its way into government networks and along the trade routes to other countries in Africa.

Ethiopia today has a large Christian presence, estimated to be nearly 60 percent of the population. Though separated by two millennia, could the dormant seeds sown long ago by this civil servant be springing to life? Jesus asked: "What is the kingdom of God like? What shall I compare it to? It is like a mustard seed, which a man took and planted in his garden. It grew and became a tree, and the birds of the air perched in its branches" (Luke 13:18-19). Likewise, might the "kingdom" seeds you plant over coffee at the work break or the compassion you extend to a fellow employee in a time of need be exactly what the Lord will nurture and bring to life?

LYDIA

Finally, we turn to a businesswoman named Lydia. We find her among a small group of women by the side of a river in the Macedonian city of Philippi. The apostle Paul and his companions have been redirected from their intended travels through Asia to this leading Roman city, their first venture into Europe. As Paul spoke, "One of those listening was a woman named Lydia, a dealer in purple cloth. . . . The Lord opened her heart to respond to Paul's message" (Acts 16:14). After she and members of her household were baptized, she persuaded Paul and the others to stay in her home. Can you imagine the crash course these new believers received, equipping them to take the gospel message into their spheres of influence on the European continent?

Three often-overlooked emissaries of the gospel: a Roman soldier, a queen's treasurer, and a merchant woman. "Everyday folks" who were available, obedient and strategically placed. Through them the gospel was propelled to the Gentiles, to Africa and to Europe. If they can do it, we can too! We can be God's ambassadors to extend his kingdom right where we are, right in the workplace.

7

Lessons from the Edge of Civilization

On the earth, nations will be in anguish and

perplexity at the roaring and tossing of the sea.

LUKE 21:25

As I've been writing this book, the world has witnessed multiplied horrendous storms and violent natural disasters. These have included a series of powerful hurricanes pounding heavily populated areas around the Caribbean and the Gulf of Mexico as well as a magnitude 7.6 earthquake that wreaked enormous destruction in Pakistan, and in parts of India and Afghanistan.

And how can we forget the tsunami that swept across the Indian Ocean on December 26, 2004? The devastation to homes, businesses and infrastructure will take years, maybe decades, to rectify, but these will be rebuilt. However, the human loss of family members, friends, neighbors and coworkers will leave jagged scars that can never be erased.

Scientists have speculated how many lives could have been saved through an effective early warning system. Likely tens of thousands, with even minutes' notice, could have moved far enough back from beaches and coastlines to assure their personal safety. But the warnings never came. No system was in place. No sirens pierced the sun-drenched skies over pristine beaches and isolated fishing villages to announce the impending doom. It was all too improbable, too sudden—and most were caught unawares.

Like the tsunami's devastating force and suddenness, coming events described by the Scriptures will bewilder, perplex and bring destruction to nations and their institutions, including business and commerce. So overwhelming will be the events that in one description, "the kings of the earth, the princes, the generals, the rich, the mighty, and every slave and every free man hid in caves and among the rocks of the mountains," even calling on the mountains and rocks to fall on them to hide them from impending judgment (Revelation 6:15-16).

AN EARLY WARNING SYSTEM

Yet in contrast to the peoples who had no warning of the tsunami, we have graciously been given a warning system by God to alert us to events that will one day affect the workplaces of the world. In this chapter we will look at the foremost of these warnings, which we find in the book of Revelation. But before we do, I want to explain how this discovery became so significant to me and why I feel it is such an important focus here.

For nearly a decade I have made it my practice to read the book of Revelation each year. With each reading, added pieces from this "mysterious" book have fallen into place, often tying into and adding significance to other parts of the Scriptures. A few years ago, I was amazed to "discover" a perspective on modern business and commerce from Revelation 18, a chapter that describes the sudden and final fall of Babylon (which many Bible scholars agree is not so much a literal city as used here but a representation of the fallen world and its systems).

I have come to view this chapter as highly significant because

- Revelation 18 is the most comprehensive chapter in the entire Bible relating specifically to business and commerce.

- it is the final chapter before the declaration of the Lord's ultimate triumph (and the wedding supper between him, the groom, and the church, the bride).

- it presents a clear, detailed set of activities for which Babylon will be judged—all of which, significantly, are present in modern businesses and business systems.

- it makes clear the Lord's position toward these condemned activities. That position is the same today as it will be in his final judgment.

- it provides clear and specific understanding of what the Lord most despises in business and commerce.

- it helps us clarify what he most values—the exact opposite of what he will judge!

- it gives hope that if we will practice what he most values, we will realize his blessings instead of his judgments.

What I've just outlined is a mouthful, and we haven't even begun to look at details of this remarkable passage. But I hope that over the next pages you will see that God is taking us "back to the future," providing practical, timely and vitally important lessons—and warnings—from the trailing edge of civilization. These lessons, as with the people featured in previous chapters, are also "companions on the journey."

THE JUDGMENTS OF BABYLON

In my careful look at Revelation 18, I noticed seven specific reasons for God's judgment of Babylon. I will note the relevant verses, cite each characteristic for which she was judged (in italics), and then suggest alternatives—remedies by which we can move out of the path of judgment into a position of blessing.

1. SPIRITUAL ABANDONMENT

After this I saw another angel coming down from heaven. He had great authority, and the earth was illuminated by his splendor. With a mighty voice he shouted: "Fallen! Fallen is Babylon the Great! *She has become a home for demons and a haunt for every evil spirit,* a haunt for every unclean and detestable bird." (Revelation 18:1-2)

Revelation 18:2, "She has become a home for demons and a haunt for every evil spirit," is a vivid picture of the results of spiritual abandonment. It describes the kind of corruption that floods in when there is nothing to prevent it, when light is absolutely overwhelmed by darkness.

Have you ever been in such an environment? I felt it strongly some years ago at the Reunion Arena in Dallas. Across the hall from the prayer conference I was attending, a rock band was setting up for that evening's concert. I had never heard of Black Sabbath, and wandered in. Over the stage they had hoisted an enormous image of Satan's face. The presence of evil was thick and foreboding. If the image could have spoken he would have said with a cunning sneer, "Wait 'til I grab hold of the kids coming in here tonight!"

Such overt expressions of evil may not be present in your workplace. But make no mistake: Scriptures are clear that a real enemy opposes us. We mustn't be naive or complacent. Given a chance, Satan would infest your place of work, making it a "home for demons and a haunt for every evil spirit."

At times we've encountered spiritual opposition at our companies. For example, several years ago a rash of small fires broke out in our main plant facility over just a few months. There was no reasonable explanation. Fortunately we were able to contain each with only minor damage resulting. The clue that we were dealing with spiritual warfare was the repeated and illogical pattern. One day, and frankly with some real annoyance that we were being "hassled" in this way, we asked any of our employees who wished to, to stay after work so we could pray about the situation. We gathered around tables in our lunchroom. Some prayed aloud, others silently. As we concluded we had a remarkable sense of peace, an assurance that God had heard our prayers. The fires? Almost as though a switch had been turned off, the fires ceased and never returned.

You and your fellow Christians may be the restraining influence in *your* workplace. God has granted us unusual power in the spiritual realm. You may recall that after Jesus sent out a group of disciples to proclaim the gospel, they returned from their travels with this victorious report: "Lord, even the demons submit to us in your name" (see Luke 10:1-3, 17). Jesus would have us exercise that power today. Your prayer, your praise and your presence as the Lord's representatives will not only retard evil but invite God's presence. Occasionally I verbalize this desire by saying, "Lord, you are welcome in our companies. Come and be pleased to dwell here."

2. EXCESS

For all the nations have drunk the maddening wine of her adulteries. The kings of the earth committed adultery with her, and *the merchants of the earth grew rich from her excessive luxuries.* (Revelation 18:3)

Dateline: Fort Lauderdale, Florida

Don Weston used to feel special cruising the world in his 100-foot yacht. Yet on a recent morning at the International Boat Show here, the retired Cincinnati businessman stood on his upper deck, overshadowed by giants.

Next door was the Corrie Lynn, a 130-foot cruiser with a king-sized Jacuzzi, five cabins, retractable plasma TV screens and twin jet skis. Down the dock was the 197-foot Alfa Four, with an indoor gym, swimming pool and helicopter pad. The talk of the show was billionaire Paul Allen's new pleasure boat, Octopus, which extends over 400 feet and has a basketball court, music studio and personal submarine. That's about to be topped by a yacht under construction in Dubai for a Saudi client. It's expected to exceed 500 feet, the size of a small cruise ship. (*The Wall Street Journal*, December 14, 2004)

I love boats. And I'm not averse to either big or fast. But the question this article begs is, "Are there limits to what is correct and responsible?" Each person must decide. Excess is not appealing to the Lord. He knows what we need and provides those needs. "Do not set your heart [on them]. . . . For the pagan world runs after all such things, and your Father knows that you need them. But seek his kingdom, and these things will be given to you as well" (Luke 12:29-31).

God is not stingy; in fact, quite the opposite. His nature and desire are to bless abundantly. After instructing on tithes and offerings, the Lord says through his prophet Malachi, "Test me in this . . . and see if I will not throw open the floodgates of heaven and pour out so much blessing that you will not have room enough for it" (Malachi 3:10).

How should God's people manage this issue? It is to neither go to excess nor mistake poverty for virtue. I believe we are to be "appropriately modest," doing what is right for our calling and circumstances. Don't be too quick to judge the scale by which another defines what is appropriate. The Lord prospers some immensely. That is his prerogative (and with those blessings comes added responsibility for wise stewardship and great generosity). Whether for an individual or an institution, the balanced walk, one of appropriate modesty, is a walk that will please the Lord.

3. CORRUPTION

Then I heard another voice from heaven say: "Come out of her, my people, so that you will not share in her sins, so that you will not receive any of her plagues; for *her sins are piled up to heaven, and God has remembered her crimes.* (Revelation 18:4-5)

Corruption and criminal activity in business in the past several years have brought down industry titans and roiled financial markets. Large, respected firms such as Enron and Arthur Andersen, once the fifth leading accounting firm in the world, have been demolished. Their demise gives us a foretaste of what will happen on a massive scale in the fall of Babylon. God states through the prophet Isaiah, "I will punish the world for its evil" (Isaiah 13:11).

The roots of corruption begin small, as when a person tests a company's financial system, looking for cracks of vulnerability. Undetected, the dishonest activity becomes more brazen and eventually spins out of control. We encountered this in one of our companies. A trusted manager began a pattern of embezzlement. Going unnoticed, the employee's initial "sins" multiplied, piling up until the point where God, in his faithfulness, "turned on the searchlight." A remedial process is underway with the individual, but great damage was done to him, his family and reputation—as well as no small loss and embarrassment to the company.

How can God's servants in the marketplace inhibit this process of decline that eventually leads to judgment? The answer lies in how we deal with sin. We *will* sin. "If we claim to be without sin, we deceive ourselves and the truth is not in us" (1 John 1:8). The problem occurs when sins, though "small," are not addressed, for they will inevitably pile up. (I imagine toy wooden blocks stacked one on another. Eventually, one additional block sends the whole pile tumbling.) Christians have a better way, and it is to deal with sin swiftly and biblically: "If we confess our sins, he is faithful and just and will forgive us our sins and purify us from all unrighteousness" (1 John 1:9).

In the language of the modern workplace, we must "keep short accounts." When we knowingly offend another, we need to move promptly to get it straight. If we take liberties with an expense account, we need to be proactive to correct it. The small lies (affectionately called "white" lies) are lies nonetheless! If we become aware of illegal activity within our organizations, we need to pray, asking for wisdom about how to intervene, and take appropriate action.

Just as the "leaven" or "yeast" of deceit can spread disease in an organization, the leaven of godliness can influence others and bring needed correction. "What shall I compare the kingdom of God to?" Jesus asked. "It is like yeast that a woman took and mixed into a large amount of flour until it worked all through the dough" (Luke 13:20-21). For example, might Enron have been spared if the company's top leaders had listened and taken remedial action when employees began speaking out about the financial and ethical anomalies they were discovering? No doubt many are still asking themselves that question.

4. PRIDE

In her heart she boasts, "I sit as queen; I am not a widow, and I will never mourn." Therefore in one day her plagues will overtake her: death, mourning and famine. She will be consumed by fire, for mighty is the Lord God who judges her. (Revelation 18:7-8)

God's response to these aspects of Babylon's degradation—her boastful, arrogant and callous character—was immediate and devastating. When sin is fully ripened, judgments can come very quickly.

In Proverbs 8:13 the Lord says, "I hate pride and arrogance." Chip Ingram, in his book *Holy Ambition*, says emphatically, "God hates pride 100% of the time." Does this "hate" fit the God of love? Yes. In fact, God's hatred of that which opposes his nature actually rounds out and completes his love in the way nighttime complements the day. Knowing his stern view of arrogance makes me all the more cautious, for I know I'm vulnerable. The insidious sin of pride is never far from infecting my heart and attitudes.

Consider how pride has brought down those in high places. Pride swelled the heart of the archangel Lucifer, prompting him to lead a cosmic rebellion against God: "You said in your heart, '*I* will ascend to heaven; *I* will raise my throne above the stars of God; *I* will sit enthroned . . . *I* will make myself like the Most High'" (Isaiah 14:13-14, italics added).

Pride brought down ancient Babylon's kings. Though King Nebuchadnezzar had been warned, he declared from the roof of his royal palace: "Is not this the great Babylon *I* have built as the royal residence, by *my* mighty power and for the glory of *my* majesty?" (Daniel 4:30, italics added). Note the "I's" and "my's" that abound when people succumb to pride, and consider how frequently we hear these dangerous personal pronouns in today's business world.

Among the wide array of self-inflicted wounds I have observed in commerce and with business leaders, the most prevalent and destructive is pride. Pride causes people to set themselves on pedestals and look down on others. Pride breeds prejudice. Pride desensitizes us to others' needs, blunting compassion. Pride deafens us to the concerns of customers and employees. Pride justifies lavish indulgence. Pride dupes people into illicit relationships, damaging marriages and families. Proverbs 16:18, frequently quoted but not often enough observed, warns of the inevitable consequence:

Pride goes before destruction,
> a haughty spirit before a fall.

Marketplace believers are called to make a difference. Our first priority is to deal with pride and walk in its direct counterpart— humility. It is no small task. (I'm amused by the story of a man who was awarded a lapel pin for being the most humble person in his church. Then the elders had to take it away because he wore it!) I find it hard to detect pride in myself. I'm often well down the road toward offending someone before I realize that self-centeredness, self-importance and self-justification have taken hold. Thankfully I can say that God will usually send someone—often with a large hatpin—to deflate my balloon!

The strongest safeguard I've found against pride is to intention-ally practice humility. As we see in 1 Peter 5:6, God wants us to take the initiative: "Humble *yourselves*, therefore, under God's mighty hand." Our prayer should not be "Lord, make me hum-ble." Humbling ourselves is *our* job.

Here are some ways to practice humility in the workplace:

- Replace the words *me, I* and *my* with *us, we* and *our*.

- Acknowledge a compliment with a simple "thank you." Don't embellish. Don't be falsely modest. Don't let it linger too long, but deflect it to the Lord and to others.

- Take the "lowest seat" (Luke 14:10-11). This wise counsel often applies in business and social situations.

- Mourn with others. Jesus said, "Blessed are those who mourn" (Matthew 5:4). Fellow employees and business associates face enormous personal challenges and warrant our empathy, love and care.

- Build safeguards. We will eventually get stung if we carelessly place ourselves in the way of temptation. Traveling with or giving private counsel to an employee of the opposite sex is an unnecessary risk. Have another person along. Be thoroughly professional in office and workplace relationships.

- Practice generosity as a lifestyle, giving circumspectly so that you never try to manipulate or seek personal attention through a gift.

In *Good to Great*, author Jim Collins comments that he was struck by the "compelling modesty" of most successful CEOs he studied, describing them as "quiet, humble, modest, reserved, shy, gracious, mild-mannered, self-effacing and understated." This isn't the typical view of top business execs. But isn't it good to know that those who are most effective are men and women with these personal attributes?

5. DEVALUING PEOPLE

The merchants of the earth will weep and mourn over her because *no one buys their cargoes any more—cargoes of gold, silver, precious stones* and pearls; fine linen, purple, silk and scarlet cloth; every sort of citron wood, and articles of every kind made of ivory, costly wood, bronze, iron and marble; cargoes of cinnamon and spice, of incense, myrrh and frankincense, of wine and olive oil, of fine flour and wheat; cattle and sheep; horses and carriages; *and bodies and souls of men.* (Revelation 18:11-13)

These verses identify nearly thirty "commodities," and the order of the list speaks volumes about why Babylon was judged. Most important to the merchants who grieved over Babylon's destruction were these: gold, silver, precious stones and pearls. Last, and of least value to them, were the bodies and souls of men.

Does this blatant inversion of worth happen in today's world of commerce? The language we use is a sobering indicator. To "hit financial targets" and "meet analysts' expectations," businesses "reduce headcount," "rationalize" and "downsize" their workforces. A search on Google for "workforce reduction" brings up an amazing 8.9 million references. "Downsizing" is referenced 2.4 million times. Is this a clue into the pervasiveness of current practices that minimize people?

Granted, businesses need to make tough decisions, and those decisions often affect people. But we must carefully measure the human toll and avoid even a passing thought that people are commodities. When people are last on the cargo list, every form of human exploitation, including slavery, will ultimately follow. How much this dishonors and even angers God who "created man in his own image" (Genesis 1:27), a breathtaking reality that affirms his deep affection for each person.

To avert God's righteous judgment and seek his favor, should we not turn upside down the cargo list in Revelation 18, putting the bodies and souls of men first and "downsizing" gold, silver and precious stones?

6. ABUSING INFLUENCE

> The light of a lamp will never shine in you again. The voice
> of bridegroom and bride will never be heard in you again.
> *Your merchants were the world's great men. By your magic spell*
> *all the nations were led astray.* (Revelation 18:23)

Babylon was judged because important leaders squandered and
abused their influence, leading entire nations astray. Whether deliberately or unwittingly, they employed evil practices in their
commercial activities. Materialism has power.

Just as materialism has power, the merchants of the world have
power—either for good or for evil. A broad survey of history indicates that beginning in the mid-twentieth century, business and
commerce became *the* dominant influences worldwide. In earlier
periods, primary influences had been the military, religion and national political powers. Indeed, there are numerous multinational
companies today with market value exceeding the GDP (gross domestic product) of countries in which they do business.

When a "merchant" abuses his or her influence, the shock
waves can be felt around the globe. For example, when Dennis
Kozlowski, ex-CEO of Tyco, was indicted for stealing $600 million
from his company, in addition to a variety of other abuses the impact rippled out to over four thousand Tyco facilities located in all
fifty states in the United States and over one hundred countries
worldwide. The impact also reached the company's thousands of
suppliers and creditors and the communities in which they were
located. Indeed, today's merchants are "great men" and often wield
enormous power.

Where these "great men" are men and women of integrity and proven character, they can positively influence trading practices in their broad spheres of influence. (By the way, Tyco's new leadership team is doing just that as they endeavor to turn this $40 billion company around.)

I am encouraged that God increasingly has his people in positions of significant influence in the corporate world. I think of a friend, Dean Borgman, who recently retired as the CEO of Sikorsky Aircraft, a manufacturer of helicopters (including the Black Hawk, used by the U.S. military). Dean had traveled to one of the smaller Middle Eastern countries to pin down specifications for approximately twelve helicopters this country planned to purchase. It was for a new model, and his company was very eager to make the sale.

Dean thought it a little strange that the first event on the schedule would be a dinner at the home of the country's military chief. His concerns proved valid. The dinner was very private—in fact, he was the only guest. After the usual complement of casual discussion and pleasantries, his host "got down to business." The military chief made it clear he would be in a position to determine who would be awarded the contract, then brazenly added that he expected to be "rewarded" in some significant way for his support.

Losing this order could ultimately cost Sikorsky hundreds of millions of dollars. But Dean knew the request violated U.S. government contracting laws, his own company's ethics policy and, most important, his own personal values. "It was something that violated every principle that I attempted to hold on to in business," he later related. So Dean graciously but firmly closed off the conversation, and his host abruptly concluded the evening's event. (The helicopter order was subsequently awarded to a European supplier.) Though Dean was understandably disappointed, he was able to sleep at night. He knew he had done the right thing. In an ironic twist, the chief of the military was removed from office not long after this incident, and Sikorsky grew in stature as an honorable company that could be trusted.

As with Dean, top execs of major companies often have unique access to the seats of power in nations throughout the world. Their wise use of influence will bring blessings not only to their companies but also to the nations they represent. What a wonderful alternative to the scene in Babylon, where judgment rained down because the "great men" led entire nations astray.

7. REJECTING GOD'S SERVANTS

In her was found *the blood of prophets and of the saints,* and of all who have been killed on the earth. (Revelation 18:24)

The seventh (and final) reason Babylon was judged is that this evil city—and the world system it represents—rejected those whom God sent. The words of Jesus come to mind as he lamented over his beloved Jerusalem: "O Jerusalem, Jerusalem, you who kill the prophets and stone those sent to you, how often I have longed to gather your children together, as a hen gathers her chicks under her wings, but you were not willing. Look, your house is left to you desolate" (Matthew 23:37-38).

A high price is paid by organizations that reject those whom God sends. The "prophets and saints" in a particular business may be hidden away in obscure jobs, or they may be in executive suites. They sometimes come in unusual packages: people who don't run with the crowd, who don't "fit" in conventional ways. They are usually people with strong commitments to their companies. They are endowed with a strong sense of right and wrong. My hunch is they're present in every organization.

At Enron, as noted in chapter three, one of those who courageously stepped forward to voice her concerns was Sherron Watkins. Watkins, a member of Houston's First Presbyterian Church, was named *Time Magazine's* "Person of the Year" in 2002—one of three "whistleblowers" who sought to correct abuse in their organizations. (The others, both women, were at WorldCom and the FBI.) Once aware of the accounting problems at Enron, Watkins looked for constructive ways to bring them to light. Eventually she met with Kenneth Lay, Enron's chairman, and detailed "an elaborate accounting hoax" going on in the company. She was essentially ignored. Months later, this huge company collapsed.

In a touch of irony, *Time* notes that when Watkins was unpacking the boxes she had taken from her Enron office, she happened upon a green sticky-note pad the firm once handed out to employees. On it was a quote from Martin Luther King Jr.: "Our lives begin to end the day we become silent about things that matter." Sherron was one who spoke up. How tragic that nobody listened.

If God brings judgment when the prophets and saints are rejected, how important that corporate leaders consciously pursue the alternative—to *welcome* those whom God sends. In my experience, this begins with prayer, asking God to direct those of his choosing into our organizations. We need to be especially discerning in the hiring process, remembering what Samuel said concerning David: "The LORD does not look at the things man looks at" (1 Samuel 16:7).

Finally, we must open the cultures of our organizations to encourage people to speak up and be heard. Multiple avenues of communication need to exist. Not everyone is prepared to meet with the company's top leadership as Sherron Watkins did. From receptive (and perceptive) supervisors to suggestion boxes to e-mail access to exec availability, we need to encourage upward communication. We need to welcome the prophets and saints.

WILL THE WARNING BE HEEDED?

How long did God wait before judging Babylon? The apostle John's account of God's outpoured wrath in Revelation suggests it was the final event of the age: "After this I heard what sounded like the roar of a great multitude in heaven shouting: 'Hallelujah! Salvation and glory and power belong to our God, for true and just are his judgments'" (Revelation 19:1-2).

This indicates to me that the Lord is exercising great restraint toward the world and its systems, particularly business. In fact, the book of Revelation opens by speaking about the "patience of Jesus Christ" (Revelation 1:9 NKJV). He wants to allow maximum time for the redemptive influence of his people to bear fruit. Eventually judgment must come, and it will be thoroughly justified. But how important that you and I not ignore the fatal flaws of a failed empire but rather steadfastly resolve to seize every opportunity to do just the opposite.

PART THREE

God's Workplace Agenda

8

Moving Beyond Principles

Then [David] took his staff in his hand [and]

chose five smooth stones from the stream.

1 SAMUEL 17:40

Everything was difficult about getting to eastern Russia. Delayed flights. Lost luggage. Computers going down. Snarled communication.

Vladivostok was headquarters for the Soviet Pacific Naval Fleet. Until a few years ago it was a closed city, even to most Russians. Today, like a rusty San Francisco, it seeks to emerge from its seventy years of desolation under communism. The challenges are huge. Seven time zones from Moscow, it is the last stop on the Trans-Siberian Railroad. In fact, the far east region of Russia, bordering China, in many ways seems more Asian than Russian.

How improbable then that a small team of us had been invited there to conduct a two-day seminar focused on a biblical approach to business—the first time for this teaching emphasis (to our knowledge) in this part of the world. How could we have ever anticipated the life-changing impact our visit would have on these people, and on us?

It was no surprise that our meeting place was a hall formerly used for Communist Party indoctrination. What *was* surprising was a turnout of 160 people, some traveling from as far as the Arctic Circle. We were amazed! A decade ago, these people could hardly have imagined a day when they would be entrepreneurs in their own businesses, immersed in capital formation, manufacturing, marketing, sales, distribution and profit generation. Now they were Russia's most eager learners, longing to enter the world arena in business and commerce. And here *we* were, invited to help. My challenge: to construct a biblical foundation under their pursuits. I decided to focus on five workplace themes, junctions where the Bible and business most clearly and powerfully intersect. I call them "God's Workplace Agenda."

Russia's newest businesspeople listened intently. They took notes. They asked tough questions. And every waking moment they discussed the application in their own lives and work. The excitement of these men and women was incredible. Toward the end of our time they resolved that they had, indeed, been *called* into the marketplace and asked for prayer to confirm their commitment. They vowed to stand strong against corruption and the myriad obstacles they face. They volunteered to be God's servants in business and commerce.

FIVE WORKPLACE THEMES

Over the years, as I've studied the Scriptures that apply to business and the professions, I've found insights that fall into two main categories. The first revolves around people and what we can learn from them—men and women from Adam to Esther, from Boaz to

Lydia—the "Companions on the Journey" discussed in previous chapters.

The second category is not person-specific but thematic: major biblical ideas relating to the workplace, themes that transcend time, circumstances and people. They are principles and patterns that permeate God's Word. Large ideas that recur and by their very repetition deserve special attention. Structural building blocks upon which policies and practices can be built. Connection points linking biblical truth to business needs. Fulcrums for greater effectiveness. They are typically not the stuff of business school curricula (though their inclusion would benefit every aspiring business leader).

The five themes on which I focus in the following pages constitute "God's Workplace Agenda." I've found from several decades in business that when my work is aligned around these themes, there are multiplied ways in which God's peace and favor are evident.

One could argue for more than five themes or settle for fewer. For myself, I've found these particular topics comprehensive and of real, practical help. As with the "five smooth stones" David used to slay his adversary, these five themes may be just what you need in your business arsenal. (Incidentally, David selected five stones in preference to King Saul's armor, which he feared would merely weigh him down. We need to take care that the plethora of popular and promising management approaches don't likewise encumber us.)

The five themes I will cover in the following chapters are

- *Purpose.* Individuals and organizations function with far greater effectiveness when they have a clear sense of purpose. Each of us needs to ask, "What am I here for?" Knowing our purpose frees us from debilitating diversions and helps us focus on what is most important.

- *Values.* Core values are like an internal gyroscope, keeping us on course. They remind us and inform others, "This is what I stand for." They define boundaries. They point us toward what is noble, good and sustainable.

- *People.* People are God's priority. When we put others ahead of ourselves we align with his agenda. A deep respect for every individual can transform the character and culture of the workplace.

- *Stewardship.* Stewardship addresses ownership. Is that for which we're responsible ours, or God's? Understanding that distinction influences our management of time, possessions and other resources. It helps us persevere through difficulties and achieve true success.

- *Serving.* A serving approach reflects the heart of Jesus, who came to serve, not to be served. Our focus on service orients us toward the needs of others, including customers and clients.

I recommend that you consider how these five themes apply to your work. Use them as reference points to keep you on target. There may even be ways to reflect them in your organization's guiding documents.

MORE THAN PRINCIPLES

These five themes are not to be construed as "formulas." I'm not convinced any formulaic approach to applying scriptural truth is adequate, though we see much of that in modern business writing. And people are receptive to it. Many, even non-Christians, believe that by simply applying a given principle or precept, "we'll get God's blessing" and results will follow automatically. To be sure, God wants to bless, but he will never allow himself to be reduced to a formula. He is not there to do our bidding like some "mascot" (a term used by David Bryant in his book *Christ Is All!*).

God works differently. Though his ways follow patterns and principles, they are neither automatic nor patently predictable, nor are they the sum total of his interaction with us. He moves by the power of his Holy Spirit and in line with his Word. He works through relationships with his people, through their surrender and obedience. He comes alongside those who seek him first. He is intent on being personally involved.

So as with our Russian friends who were so challenged and helped during our days together, and with their commitment to serve God in the marketplace still ringing in my ears, let us look more closely at God's Workplace Agenda.

9

The Power of Purpose

Effective CEOs pick two tasks and devote their energies there.
When those tasks are done, they don't go to #3. They make a new list.

PETER DRUCKER

In accomplishing anything definite a man renounces everything else.

GEORGE SANTAYANA

The day our company faced its greatest threat was the day we lost focus.

To understand our predicament, I need to take you back a few years, actually to the founding. Challenges in those early years were intense, enough to sink many fledgling businesses.

The company was undercapitalized from its start in 1937. Earlier, my dad had lost his savings in the Great Depression and therefore had to begin the new business on a shoestring. He brought in a business partner with some modest capital in exchange for half ownership in the company. Expensive equity! But it was necessary to get going.

The business was just a few years old when World War II broke out. As I mentioned in an earlier chapter, it soon became impossible to produce our core product because of parts shortages. In response, Dad took the company in a new direction for the next several years—insulating homes. This step, though a major departure from the core business, enabled the company not only to survive but to keep all its employees working.

After the War, the company returned to its original mandate—producing oil burners for use in heating homes, schools, churches and small businesses. Production ramped up quickly. In fact, by the early fifties results were strong enough that Dad surprised the family by purchasing a Chrysler sedan, our first new car in ten years. Then, right in the midst of our growing prosperity, an ominous new threat emerged. I was in college at the time, engrossed in my world—unaware of my father's crisis. Only later did I learn what happened. Only later did I find out about the day we lost our sense of purpose.

THE DAY WE LOST PURPOSE

Heating oil was a readily available fuel source in the early years of our business. Natural gas, which now dominates residential heating, was deemed of little value. As a byproduct of crude oil production, gas was flared off (burned in the open atmosphere) at the wellhead. But in time, producers began capturing this "waste byproduct" and transporting it into major Midwest cities through a new network of pipelines. Large-scale conversions to this inexpensive, plentiful fuel became a common occurrence.

My dad resigned himself to a somber conclusion: the heating oil industry would never be able to compete with natural gas. It would only be a matter of time before this competitive threat would sink his young business. That was the day the company lost focus.

In his discouragement, Dad decided to plow our modest surplus cash into—of all things—asbestos mines in Canada. Soon the now legendary health concerns with asbestos burst into public view, and with frightening speed his investments became worthless. The company, now stripped of cash, just about went under.

Eventually Dad put this poor decision behind him and painstakingly began updating and improving the company's core products. Some markets remained strong, especially in the Northeast where there was less of a competitive threat from natural gas. In time, the company inched its way back to profitability with steadily improving technology. One of Dad's friends later told me that when my father took this step back to "the basics," his enthusiasm returned and he worked toward the future with a tremendous burst of energy.

In the ensuing years, the company would face other challenges, some of them formidable. But none exceeded the peril presented by that day, the day the Beckett Corporation lost its sense of direction—the day we lost purpose.

THE LESSON LEARNED

I wish I'd had a good "fireside chat" with my dad at some point about this difficult chapter in his otherwise successful business career. I never did. Had that occurred, I imagine he would have said something like this:

> John, I began this business to provide clean, convenient and
> affordable heat to people in cold climates. I remember like it
> was yesterday shoveling coal into our furnace as I was grow-

ing up. By the mid-1920s, people recognized oil heating was a big improvement over coal. It was cleaner and it was automatic. No more shoveling! It was really a great technical advance. I was enthused enough about the future of oil heating that when I had a chance to go into business for myself, I wanted nothing more than to design and produce the world's finest oil burners.

But after some initial success, I let a threat from another fuel source cloud my thinking. I lost sight of our purpose and became discouraged. That kept me from seeing untapped opportunities within our core business. Finally, I realized we could make adjustments in our products and marketing strategy and continue a vital role in fulfilling our original purpose.

THE POWER OF PURPOSE

When an individual or a business finds and maintains its purpose, the impact can be enormous. Purpose causes that which was once disordered, fragmented and out of harmony to become focused, cohesive, ordered and exciting.

Have you ever listened to a symphony orchestra warming up? You'd think you were listening to cats fighting! Violins and clarinets scurry aimlessly up and down the scales; trumpets and trombones blast pompous noises; drums and cymbals bang and clatter—all part of the routine as the orchestra's musicians limber fingers, moisten reeds and flex their musical muscles. (The random sounds are not unlike the cacophony heard in some modern-day organizations.)

The first hint of order occurs when the conductor points to the oboist, who issues a plaintive "A," the note to which the different instruments are tuned. Musicians make final adjustments. Then a hush falls. The stage and audience become eerily silent. Every eye is fixed on the maestro. He raises his baton, and on the first down-beat—music! Harmony! Energy! Purpose! With one stroke of the conductor's baton that which was random becomes focused, strategic. A hundred people are working together, depending on each other to accomplish a common goal.

Such is the kind of harmony worthy of your life and the life of your organization. Such is the nature and transforming power of purpose.

WHERE PURPOSE ORIGINATES

Rick Warren's bestseller *The Purpose-Driven Life* boldly states, "It is only in God that we discover our origin, our identity, our meaning, our purpose, our significance, and our destiny. Every other path leads to a dead end" (p. 18).

Warren contrasts this God-centered view with popular self-focused approaches. "Self-help books, even Christian ones, usually offer the same predictable steps to finding your life's purpose: . . . Clarify your values. Set some goals. Figure out what you're good at. Aim high."

While there may be some validity to these overworked approaches, the Bible assures us from a God-centered perspective, our heavenly Father has plans and purposes for us that transcend the best that we can concoct on our own. For example, the prophet Jeremiah wrote to a nation in captivity, "'I know the plans

I have for you,' declares the LORD, 'plans to prosper you and not to harm you, plans to give you hope and a future'" (Jeremiah 29:11). And the psalmist offers this petition:

> May He grant you according to your heart's *desire,*
> And fulfill all your purpose. (Psalm 20:4 NKJV)

These remarkable expressions of God's care, I believe, extend broadly and apply to each person, and even to every organization, institution, community and nation. He has a purpose for you. He has a purpose for your company.

EVIDENCE IN MY LIFE

Each of us has a story that reveals God's unique purpose in our lives. My story begins with the improbability that I am even here to tell about it.

It was a miracle that my father survived World War I. For three years he fought on the front lines with the Canadian infantry, mainly in France. It the midst of the enormous toll of human destruction in that war, only Dad and one other man in his company of over eighty men survived. God obviously had a purpose for him beyond the battle lines in France.

My parents were married in 1933, and their first child was a daughter. Something went wrong at her birth (apparently a medical error), and she died. So distressed were my father and mother that they seriously considered not having any more children. But God had a purpose, and a few years later, in 1938, I was born, followed by two sisters.

I became very ill at a young age. But a "miracle drug" called penicillin was in early trials, and, at some risk, I was treated with it. The penicillin was effective and my life was spared. God had a purpose and he made a way.

I've already mentioned many of the defining moments in my life: choice of college, meeting Wendy, a "call" to business, joining my father in his company, coming into a vital relationship with Christ. All these are hard evidence of the hand of a loving God, meticulously weaving together the fabric of my life. When I have strayed from his plans—and I often have—he has faithfully and lovingly brought me back to himself, all for the fulfillment of his purposes. I have not a shadow of doubt that the verse from Jeremiah is true: "I know the plans I have for you."

GOD'S PLANS FOR YOUR LIFE

Our heavenly Father knows the plans he has for *you* as well. They are deliberately woven into a design much larger than you or I can imagine.

Here's a helpful exercise. Take inventory of how God has been active in your life. Write out a list of all the ways you have seen him at work. I did this several years ago, and the process was very revealing. I saw his involvement in ways that had previously escaped my notice. You will discover the same. You could even encourage family members, friends or colleagues to comment on how they've seen God shaping and directing your life. They may well think of things you might not recall on your own.

PURPOSE IN JESUS' LIFE

Jesus was the ultimate "Purpose-Driven" leader. He knew what he was called to do and, at the end of his life, declared that he had completely fulfilled that calling.

He was crystal clear that his overarching purpose was to do the Father's will: "For I have come down from heaven not to do my will but to do the will of him who sent me" (John 6:38). Then he stated his Father's will: "that everyone who looks to the Son and believes in him shall have eternal life" (John 6:40). Combined, these clear declarations powerfully summarize Jesus' purpose in coming to earth: He came down from heaven in order that everyone who looks to him and believes in him would have eternal life.

As Jesus began his brief period of active ministry, he translated this large purpose into specifics, a kind of "plan of implementation." Speaking in Nazareth, he cited several objectives: "The Spirit of the Lord is on me, because he has anointed me to preach good news to the poor. He has sent me to proclaim freedom for the prisoners and recovery of sight for the blind, to release the oppressed, to proclaim the year of the Lord's favor" (Luke 4:18-19). For the next three years Jesus pursued these goals with singular focus.

Imagine how easily Jesus could have strayed off course. (By current standards it would have been justified, if not applauded.) He could have addressed pressing political challenges or kicked off an expansive ministry organization. Why not establish teaching centers, write books or at least publish a newsletter? And what about his decision to limit his immediate circle to twelve? So small a group for such a great leader and mission.

Yet had Jesus been deflected from his primary focus, he would have missed the mark. The consequences of even a "near miss" are unfathomable to contemplate. Anything short of the cross would have deprived you and me of the greatest gift ever given—a clear path back to the Father.

How resolute was Jesus to fulfill his mission? Mark comments on the final trek up to Jerusalem: "They were on their way up to Jerusalem, with Jesus *leading the way*, and the disciples were astonished, while those who followed were afraid" (Mark 10:32, italics added). Here was Jesus, the only one in the crowd who knew what lay ahead, and he was at full stride out ahead of them. Isaiah tells us he had set his face "like flint" (Isaiah 50:7). What a picture of determination!

Jesus achieved the Father's purpose with such fidelity that he was able to say at the close of his life, "I have brought you glory on earth by *completing* the work you gave me to do" (John 17:4, italics added). Think about that for a moment. What about all the people who *weren't* healed, who *didn't* hear his life-giving message or who heard but weren't convinced? Wasn't there much unfinished business?

Yet in the context of the purpose for which he came, Jesus was able to say his work was complete. I find this breathtaking, and also encouraging that we too can come to the point where his purposes for our lives are fulfilled and our work on earth is complete.

Rick Warren confirms the power of such focus. He asserts that we need a clear understanding of purpose, not so we can cram more activities into already crowded schedules, but rather that we might do *less* in life—focusing on what matters most. "It's about becoming what *God* created you to be" (p. 19).

PURPOSE IN JESUS' FOLLOWERS

The book of Acts reveals the clarity of purpose that guided the early church. An example occurred early, just after Pentecost. Peter and John were arrested after healing a man who had been crippled from birth. Even under threat of execution, they boldly declared, "Judge for yourselves whether it is right in God's sight to obey you rather than God. For we cannot help speaking about what we have seen and heard" (Acts 4:19-20). Their overriding imperative was to declare and demonstrate the power of God they had witnessed.

Stephen, appointed as one of seven deacons, did "great wonders and miraculous signs among the people," and paid for his singular focus with his life (Acts 6:8). But God had a purpose. From his death and the ensuing persecution, the church was scattered and the gospel thrust outward to the "ends of the earth" (Acts 8:1; see also Acts 1:8).

Likewise the apostle Paul, from the time of his conversion, held fast to his Damascus Road commissioning: "I am sending you to them (the Gentiles) to open their eyes and turn them from darkness to light, and from the power of Satan to God, so that they may receive forgiveness of sins" (Acts 26:17-18). If you are a Gentile, you are a direct beneficiary of Paul's full obedience to that laser-sharp call.

We in the workplace should seek the same clarity of purpose the early disciples had. Did focus akin to Stephen's compel the nineteenth-century reformer William Wilberforce, "a man who changed his times" (John Pollock, in Os Guinness, *Character Counts*, p. 77), to press through monstrous barriers to end slavery in England? Or did zeal to proclaim the message of God's redemption energize George Frideric Handel to compose the *Messiah* in 1741 in a mere twenty-four days? Whether we are driving social reform or composing music, serving customers or cooking the evening meal, God calls us to pursue his will and purpose for us.

WHEN PURPOSE HITS PROBLEMS

The clearer the purpose, the more sharply it will be contested. It's as though our enemies, visible and invisible, see a bull's-eye painted on our backs. Nehemiah wasn't a threat until he started to rebuild (Nehemiah 2:17-19). Daniel could have avoided the lion's den had he not "got down on his knees and prayed" as was his habit (Daniel 6:10). Stephen might have avoided death by stoning, if, while recounting Israel's history before the Sanhedrin, he had moderated his speech instead of describing his accusers as "stiff-necked people" bent on resisting the Holy Spirit (Acts 7:51).

Count on it. When we doggedly pursue a noble purpose, it will make people furious. But just as God is in our purpose, he's also present in our problems. Nehemiah's resistance to his detractors galvanized Jerusalem's inhabitants around their mission. Daniel's survival in the lions' den so profoundly affected the king that he issued a decree "that in every part of my kingdom people must fear and reverence the God of Daniel" (Daniel 6:26). And greatest of all, Jesus' death by crucifixion—the world's greatest tragedy—resulted in history's greatest triumph.

Admittedly it's hard to see God's larger agenda when we're in the midst of the problem. But there is always a larger drama playing out. I didn't see it in my father's untimely death or in the fire that followed. But the impact of those events drove me closer to God and eventually into a vital relationship with Christ. I didn't see it in the midst of a labor union's attempt to organize our workforce.

But wrestling with that reality helped us fashion major changes in our attitudes and policies toward our employees. I didn't see it when our company was thrust into a national spotlight by the ABC News story. But the positive reaction it generated propelled me into my current focus—to encourage others with what God is doing in the marketplace.

Though we see only in part, we can be certain God is at work. He is faithful to bring forth his purposes, often in ways and at times we don't expect. It is so reassuring to know that even when storm clouds threaten, when things seem most difficult, we can trust him. Indeed, he *does* work all things together for good—to those who love him and are called according to *his purpose* (see Romans 8:28).

WORKPLACE PURPOSE

Clarity of purpose is important for organizations but also for work groups and even each of us as individuals. Within organizations, those in senior leadership have primary responsibility for defining the organization's purpose. In looking through purpose statements from companies I know and admire, some stand out for their clarity and tone.

C. P. Morgan Company builds some three thousand homes each year in the Indianapolis area. Chuck Morgan, the CEO, is a highly principled Christian who wants faith to influence every aspect of his company's work. Morgan's goal for his business: "To provide more people with more home than they ever dreamed possible" (www.cpmorgan.com).

Auntie Anne's irresistible pretzels are available around the world. (Their mere mention gets people's mouths watering!) As former CEO, Anne Beiler spearheaded the company's broad purpose to be a "shining LIGHT in the business community." They will:

Lead by example
Invest in employees
Give freely
Honor God
Treat everyone with integrity

In a world that is cynical about business greed, here is Auntie Anne's mission: "Our profits will be invested to help others develop their greatest potential, and to maintain our position as the innovative leader in the marketplace. We strive to make everything we do pay tribute to God who has entrusted us with this task" (www.auntieannes.com).

Many organizations are playing "catch up" developing statements of purpose. I can empathize. Our company was lacking in this regard even after we had been in business for decades. One of our outside directors pointed out this deficiency, and we got to work forging a statement of vision. (I developed the first draft, and then our senior managers got involved in fine-tuning it.) We state:

Our vision is to build a family of exceptional companies—each of which serves its customers in distinctive and important ways—and each of which reflects the practical application of biblical values throughout.

This statement has served us well, helping us focus our people toward excellence, staying postured toward service, adding value

The Power of Purpose

for our customers and embracing high standards. Financial goals are not the primary driver. Yet as we've walked out our vision, we've prospered in ways I never would have anticipated.

Maybe your company has a statement of purpose, but it's not a good one. Might your influence bring improvement? Even a person "down the ranks" can inject inspired thinking into his or her organization by thoughtfully advancing alternate ideas. I recall some years ago that a major U.S. automotive manufacturer's stated goal for the year was to move one notch higher on *Fortune* magazine's list of the largest 500 companies. Noble? No, tepid! And perhaps an opportunity for some among the troops to suggest a loftier target.

Suppose you head a department or work team. Might you muster your people's aspirations and establish a purpose statement for your group? For example: "Our customer service department is committed to coordinating our company's resources to provide complete customer satisfaction." Or a human resources department might say, "Our purpose is to promote an environment of trust, open communication, opportunity and enthusiasm among all our employees."

PURPOSE FOR EACH PERSON

Just as clarifying purpose helps organizations and their subunits, each of us as individuals can benefit by thinking through the primary focus in our lives. Let me state mine, as an example. It is to *serve the Lord as a husband and father and extend his kingdom in the marketplace.* My wife, Wendy, sees her life as *a pouring out of worship to the Lord, and to love and intercede for me, our family, the church, the Jews and all people.* As our lives are pulled to and fro,

Wendy and I often return to these basic ideas to help us focus our time and energy most productively.

How does clarifying your purpose help? Suppose you're a violinist in a symphony orchestra? Some might say you're there just to crank out the notes, but you might take a larger view, seeing your musical gift as a wonderful expression of God's creativity. (Is it not he who has given song, instrumental creativity and inspired music to his followers throughout the ages?) Such an enlarged perspective can make getting out of bed in the morning and heading off to "work" a very different experience.

Can a person working in a manufacturing plant have a noble sense of purpose? Let me tell you about Mary. Though small in stature, physically frail and suffering from diabetes, Mary was *called* to assembly work in our company. She was on time and very dependable. She had a radiant smile and personal dignity in speech and conduct. Her greatest asset, though, was her care for others. She was always willing, if asked, to tell about the Lord she loved. And many wanted to know. As needs arose and situations compelled, Mary was always there. Ultimately this was Mary's mission. She found her purpose helping the people with whom she worked to experience the love of her Savior.

Rick Warren asks, "What on earth am I here for?" Finding the answer can be the key to all God has for you in the future. I encourage you to ask that question for yourself, in your work and in whatever spheres God has placed you.

Master your Mondays by finding your purpose!

10

Values

Courage is contagious. When a brave man takes a stand,
the spines of others are often stiffened.

BILLY GRAHAM

The last problem Archie Dunham expected to deal with was a crisis at one of his company's major construction projects. But because he was chairman and CEO of Conoco, Inc., the dilemma had landed with a thud on his desk. Two workers had been fired for flagrantly violating the company's safety standards. In protest, the entire work force had gone out on strike. Their demand? Unless the two workers were rehired, none of the employees would return to work.

As substantial as Conoco's financial commitments are in countries where they have facilities, they have an even stronger commitment to their core values, stated as follows:

At Conoco, everything we do is guided by our core values of safety, environmental stewardship, valuing all people and maintaining high ethical standards. These core values are woven into our culture. They are fundamental to sustainability and to our vision of being recognized around the world as a truly great company.

At issue was the conflict between three factors: the disruption and cost of shutting down a major construction project, the value the company placed on its workers in each country where it did business, and the importance of maintaining the company's values, especially the emphasis on safety. Dunham considered the facts, contemplated the likely implications and concluded that the company's priorities were correct. With all due respect to the cultural sensitivities of the country where the new plant was being built, the safety of their employees was their primary consideration. Unless their safety standards were upheld, the entire facility and all its employees would be in jeopardy. He concluded, "We will not rehire those two people."

A SURPRISE VISIT

A few weeks after that decision, and with the stand-off unresolved, the president of the country in which the company was located came to visit Mr. Dunham at Conoco's headquarters in Houston. He told Dunham how powerful the union was in his country and that Conoco needed to relent on rehiring the two individuals. "It would be best for Conoco, for the union and for our country."

"Mr. President," Dunham replied, "you need to understand one thing. We stand behind the core values of our company. One of those important values is the safety of our people. These two men jeopardized the safety of their fellow employees. Because they did, we fired them—and we will not hire them back."

Dunham continued. "Mr. President, I would like you to take this message back to the union: We will not rehire those workers even if we have to stop construction. This is how important our values are to us."

Within two weeks the entire workforce was back on the job—*less* the two workers. The message was clear: Conoco's core values were not negotiable.

Could this adherence to principle be one of the reasons Conoco (now Conoco-Phillips) is one of the nation's most admired and highest-performing companies (*Business Week,* April 4, 2005)? Could it be a factor in their remarkable success during a period of turmoil in the energy sector?

WHY CORE VALUES?

The Bible does not use the term *values* in the sense it is used most frequently today. The closest equivalent would be in measuring human worth, as in Matthew 10:31: "So don't be afraid; you are worth more ["of more value," NKJV] than many sparrows."

Historically the primary dictionary definition of *values* was economic: "the worth of a thing in money or goods at a certain time; market price." More recent dictionaries expand the use: "A principle, standard or quality considered worthwhile or desirable." Or in another: "that which is desirable or worthy of esteem for its own sake; thing or quality having intrinsic worth."

Modern organizations have moved steadily toward having defined "values." In Western cultures the need has become increasingly apparent as we have moved away from "traditional values" rooted in the Judeo-Christian ethic. Stephen Covey, the respected author of *The Seven Habits of Highly Effective People,* believes from his study of this subject that the shift took place after World War I.

At that time our nation began a swing from what he calls the Character Ethic (things like integrity, humility, courage, justice and the Golden Rule) to the Personality Ethic (techniques, quick fixes, "social Band-Aids and aspirin").

Sadly our culture has become increasingly untethered from our ethical and moral roots. We have redefined and exalted concepts such as tolerance and pluralism to such a degree that what was once considered absolute is deemed archaic and irrelevant. In contrast, as Os Guinness points out in *The Call,* "The Puritans lived as if they had swallowed gyroscopes." I love that imagery—the idea that our forebears had internal, faith-based stabilizers that governed their thoughts and actions and kept them on course.

The Puritans were steeped in the Scriptures. They would have understood that the Ten Commandments, for example, were never annulled but that their truths are enduring. The Ten were the "values" of their day: honoring and worshiping God only, not misusing his name, keeping the Sabbath, respect for parents, keeping oneself from murder, adultery, theft, covetousness, and bearing false testimony. These became the cultural compass for much of civilization's long history (see Exodus 20). For instance, Blackstone's Commentaries from the 1760s, the basis for our legal system, were thoroughly rooted in God's law. The impulse to found many of our great universities, establish hospitals and provide care for the poor and needy grew out of a biblical perspective.

Properly understood, the current corporate emphasis on core values is an effort to apprehend and apply those seminal ideas that have shaped the best of our culture and stood the test of time. They declare, at least within a specific organization, "These are the guidelines by which we will conduct and govern ourselves. This is our effort to define our culture."

Is this a proper emphasis? As we observed with Conoco, holding to core values is vital. Mr. Dunham's deep commitment to *safety* not only enabled the company to work through a highly charged confrontation but also sent a clear message to the entire company. He is a great example of how top leaders shape the character of the organizations they lead. If they don't, their companies will fall victim to an inherent gravitational pull toward society's lowest common denominator. Since that denominator is all too often being molded by an "agenda" that is blatantly antibiblical, and voiced through mainstream cultural megaphones such as TV and higher education, we must be all the more vigilant to hold to the definition cited earlier: "principles, standards or qualities considered worthwhile or desirable."

Core values have further benefits.

- They define what make organizations *distinctive*—desirable places to work and with whom to do business.

- They are a powerful driver for *change*, calling people to a higher standard (the high jumper's bar we raise still higher).

- They are a proper *constraint,* one leading to liberty, for when people know what an organization stands for, they are free to make independent decisions within that defined context. They know the boundaries and are confident others equally committed to those values will back them up.

- They help shape *corporate culture,* and thus influence organizational effectiveness. Dr. Daniel Denison, formerly a professor at the University of Michigan School of Business Administration, has found through extensive studies that corporate culture strongly influences bottom-line performance, including profit, market share, return on investment, sales and growth. (*Corporate Culture and Organizational Effectiveness,* Dr. Daniel Denison)

Core values needn't be trendy. Their effectiveness is often marked by their durability and simplicity, such as the core values of the U.S. Marine Corps: Honor, Courage, Commitment. These have remained unchanged for the Corps' illustrious history, dating back to 1773. General Charles Krulak, who retired as Marine Corps Commandant in 1999, found that today's young recruits respond well to clear, defined expectations. "Define the playing field, and within those boundaries they will perform magnificently," Krulak says. That reality is transferable to all organizations today and should encourage us that we both can and should define and mold corporate culture based on strong, clear values.

OUR EXPERIENCE

We have found in our companies that our people, from directors to data entry personnel, strongly support our three core values: Integrity, Excellence and Profound Respect for the Individual. All are traceable to biblical roots, giving them an enduring quality. All lend themselves to teaching and modeling. All provide ongoing accountability, even for top management.

I'll never forget a plant floor employee who drove this point home for me. He came into my office one day and respectfully suggested our management had violated one of our core values. He had my attention! "I was passed over for a promotion," Mark said. "But that isn't what bothered me. I think the company lacked respect for me when I found out what happened through the grapevine. I was off on medical leave, and within hours of the decision, several of my fellow employees called me at home to tell me I'd been passed over." "Mark, I'll look into it and get back to you," I assured him.

Normally we're very careful to visit personally with each employee who has applied for a promotion, successful or not. In this case we hadn't. Digging into the situation, I found our plant management had discussed the matter and decided it would be "more compassionate" not to call Mark at home, recovering as he was from surgery. In retrospect, it was the wrong choice between two competing values. Mark and I met to follow up and got it completely clear. He left my office smiling, and I grinned with deep satisfaction. Our core values had so thoroughly permeated the organization that an hourly employee felt free to boldly put his concerns on the table and work toward resolution, not bury them in resentment.

WHAT VALUES?

Once an organization is committed to establishing core values, it is no small task to identify which, specifically, are most appropriate. They need to reflect the hearts of people in senior leadership, for they will be their primary advocates. Some companies may need to consider how their values are viewed by others, including board members, shareholders, stock analysts and the general public. At times, concern about offending, drawing criticism or even encountering organized opposition can cause values to be so watered down they become of little or no use. "Values" such as "maximizing profit," "increasing market share" and "improving society" fall into this category. Indeed, not all values are equal.

Is there an ideal in choice of values? Where possible, an organization should reach toward values that align with biblically based concepts. Terms to consider might include service, honesty, ethical conduct, honor, family, individual worth, self-discipline, accountability. Such values have staying power. Placing them "front and center" and living them out is a practical way of bringing a little of God's kingdom closer to our daily lives.

I reviewed the values statements of a number of companies both private and public where there has been a Christian leadership influence. I was surprised and encouraged by their scope, creativity and, in many cases, their reflection of God's patterns.

VALUES WITH SUBSTANCE

Integrity. "Our actions will reflect our absolute commitment to ethical and honest behavior. When faced with uncertainty we will always use our best judgment to do the 'RIGHT THING.'"—Alaska Airlines

Growth. "Growth is important and desirable. It usually implies that we are properly responding to the needs of the marketplace."—Cass Bank and Trust Company

Diversity. "We value different points of view. Men and women from different races, cultures, and backgrounds enrich the generation and usefulness of these different points of view."—Eastman Chemical

Profit. "Profit is not the purpose of our business and should not be sought after for its own sake. Rather, it is a necessity if we are to be able to continue to deliver value to our clients."—A. G. Edwards and Sons, Inc.

Continuous improvement. "Continuous Improvement is the driving force in everything we do, and is the responsibility of every individual in the company."—Emerson Motor Company

Personal balance. "We encourage and support balanced lives and recognize that families are important to that balance."—Fresh Express

Change. "We believe that change is a way of life; we should welcome it, we should look forward to it; we should create and force change. We should not wait to react to change created by others."—Gordon Food Service

Respect for people. "We value each person's intrinsic worth and uniqueness. We acknowledge everyone's contribution and honor his/her opinions. Our work environment is open, honest, supportive and fulfilling. Our Company is built on trust."—Graphic Packaging Corporation

Responsibility. "Taking responsibility nurtures the desire to excel and allows team members to grow as individuals."—GuideOne Insurance.

Moral and ethical absolutes. "Moral and ethical absolutes do not exist outside of the context of a Supreme Being, Creator, God. With moral and ethical absolutes, God's directions and guidelines, there is stability and purpose. Without moral and ethical absolutes, there is confusion, instability and meaningless existence. Therefore, the guiding principles of our Company have their root in God's unchanging laws and directions from which there is no compromise."—Metokote Corporation

These statements from major companies should encourage us that it *is* possible to anchor guiding principles in enduring ideas. For example, when Alaska Airlines speaks about employees using their best judgment to do the "right thing," they credit their employees with having an intrinsic sense of right and wrong, encouraging them to use it.

In another example, Cass Bank and Trust extols the importance of growth. Growth is actually a reflection of the nature of a creator God who watches over an expanding universe and is willing to entrust more and more to those who follow him.

Finally, Metokote is very clear (some would say bold) in describing the basis for their core values. They link these values directly to God's unchanging laws and in so doing, bring his kingdom a little closer to earth. What a grand and welcome aspiration for any workplace.

How Far Do I Press It?

Stephen Resch, an associate professor at Indiana Wesleyan University in Fort Wayne, Indiana, wrestles with questions of conflicting values, as many of us do. He asks: "Can you as CEO require employees to live up to some absolute standard just because you say so, when the surrounding culture is relativistic and pragmatic?" Tough question. My answer is yes, at least where the standard indeed has an absolute quality. Such standards as honesty and ethical conduct don't have "wiggle room."

I agree that today's culture is "relativistic and pragmatic." Yet I believe it is incumbent on leadership to define the subculture of their organizations, to say, "This is who we are. This is what we believe. This is our expected behavior." Whether it is the Marine Corps, a professional football team, Dow Chemical or even the U.S. Government, the external culture should not dictate the standards. Leadership should. (By analogy, parents need to set the subculture of their homes. The claim that "everyone else is doing it" shouldn't cut any ice.)

I believe it is imperative for those in *leadership* to follow and model corporate values. (Otherwise leaders would be hypocritical in expecting others to observe them.) Senior executives, department heads and managers all represent management. They must "buy into" and walk out their organization's values. In our own companies we hold unswervingly to such expectations of those in leadership and take their alignment with our values into account as a key aspect of evaluating their performance.

What about those not in leadership? Greater "bandwidth" is necessary in certain areas, but not the essential core values. For example, we don't hold nonleaders to the same standard in certain areas of personal conduct such as living arrangements and lifestyles. But we have zero latitude for conduct that is dishonest or insubordinate.

Resch also asks, "In a pluralistic society, should tolerance have limits? What would that look like in the (company) manual?" Tolerance *must* have limits. Whether in a family or a company, we should be able to say, "This I will tolerate, but that I cannot." In Conoco's situation with their construction project, they were adamant in not "tolerating" safety violations. Safety trumped the individual freedom of the two employees who conducted themselves in an unsafe manner. The company manual can allow for diversity while outlining expectations that are non-negotiable. Where individual views clash with the defined values of the company, the company's values must be observed.

A final question (there could be many more) on conflicting values comes from a gentleman in Tulsa, Oklahoma. It squarely addresses an issue that is more and more pressing. "How do you work effectively with homosexual customers/coworkers? My company is 'inclusionary,' which means they accept anyone regardless of race, gender, sexual orientation, religion, etc. Many of these individuals have morals that directly conflict with my values, which causes tension or caution. How can you effectively work and be a blessing in this environment?"

It's almost impossible to not be aware of profound conflicts in society around issues of sexual orientation, not to mention religious convictions, rights of the unborn, cloning, embryonic stem-cell research and other moral/ethical challenges. Cultures are colliding in fierce ways, in our personal and corporate lives. We can't always choose our coworkers or customers, nor can we dodge the ethical and moral issues of our day. At times we're face to face with them.

How would you counsel the person in the workplace dilemma described above? After all, we may not have the first clue of what is really going on in another person's life or how the Lord may be working. But it is reassuring that God knows each person's situation intimately:

For a man's ways are in full view of the LORD,
 and he examines all his paths. (Proverbs 5:21)

This gives us confidence to ask him for wisdom; in fact, this is *always* the best starting point.

I have found that God's Word can bring great clarity when values seem to be in conflict. Psalm 85:10, for example, illustrates how two different aspects of God's nature converge: "Mercy and truth have met together" (NKJV). (I'm amused as I imagine these two powerful "personalities" having a good chat over a cup of coffee!)

Sometimes in addressing workplace difficulties I've leaned overboard to extend mercy, yet avoided delivering the necessary dose of truth. At other times I've been all truth, resulting in a void of needed compassion. Jesus had the amazing capacity to bring mercy and truth, compassion and accountability together, resulting in a graceful and effective balance. Consider the example in which the woman caught in adultery was flung before him. He turned the explosive confrontation into a powerful demonstration of the Father's love, expressed as mercy joined with truth.

Mercy: "If any one of you is without sin, let him be the first to throw a stone at her." (John 8:7)

Then, after the crowd sheepishly retreated, Jesus turned to the woman and admonished her.

Truth: "Go now and leave your life of sin." (John 8:11)

As we closely follow Jesus, we too will find ways to speak truth while extending his mercy, grace and love.

USING YOUR INFLUENCE

Are you in a position to set policy in your organization? If so, consider how you might watch over the development of employee policies and procedures. Policies are often the riverbanks where, left unattended, the company's culture erodes. For example, many large businesses today have granted "domestic partner benefits" to their employees, extending health and other benefits beyond spouses to "partners," with all that can imply. Often management has accepted a consultant's recommendation or ceded to a pressure group and given little thought to whether such an extension is really in the interests of the entire organization, or whether it may actually encourage lifestyles that are contrary to God's ways. But in some organizations there have been "watchmen" who have taken a reasoned but firm approach to keep such policies from being implemented, yet still safeguarding the deep respect that is due every individual.

If you're not in a position of direct influence, there is still much you can do. There may be times you need to directly challenge policies, even at personal risk. Recall this is exactly what Esther did, prompting a remarkable turn of events. You can think through and find ways to live out and apply corporate values in your specific area of responsibility. "Subsets" of corporate values can be adopted, such as requiring precision and accuracy in an accounting department or fostering innovation in a design function. And if company values are not biblical, you can still use your influence to apply more biblical values in your immediate sphere. This was the course Daniel and his friends took in Babylon's faith-hostile environment. There can even be a "trickle-up" effect—where a part influences the whole, especially when such an approach results in a department or work unit achieving visibly stronger performance.

Finally, never limit the power of prayer as well as Spirit-led action. "The eyes of the LORD range throughout the earth to

strengthen those whose hearts are fully committed to him"
(2 Chronicles 16:9). You could be set precisely where you are to
represent the Lord's interests.

MAKING VALUES LIVE

Developing an organization's statement of values means little unless it is communicated broadly and deeply. And that's hard work.
Values must be lived by leadership—the most powerful means of
teaching. They also must be regularly discussed and deeply em-
bedded. (Underscoring this point, I was sobered to read in a news
article that once-mighty Enron professed essentially the same core
values as those in our company.)

We can help make values live as we create and encourage corporate cultures that welcome and reinforce those values. This can
involve recognition and rewards for actions that reflect a commitment to corporate values. And it can also involve removing structural or systemic barriers to implementing values, such as unnecessary or bureaucratic processes or procedures.

A focus on our values is a regular theme at our company meetings. Occasionally we have taken employees off-site to train on
those values in greater detail. We like to get people involved in the
process. For example, we once put this challenge to our employees at a company meeting: "Our management went up a mountain
and came down with three core values: Integrity, Excellence, and
A Profound Respect for the Individual. We would like YOU to
form teams and come up with ideas on how we can make them
live." They took the assignment seriously, and on Values Day rolled
out their creative ideas. Everyone was issued a T-shirt emblazoned

with our three values. A banner was stretched across the ceiling of our manufacturing area stating:

> Let Beckett employees be known throughout the world by a commitment to living their values: Integrity • Excellence • Profound Respect for the Individual

They created a board game to help us align our values with our actions. The core values appeared on name badges and e-mail headers. It was great fun, and it was also effective in driving home the message: Values mean only as much as our willingness to internalize them and live them out.

Don't leave corporate culture to chance, regardless of your position in the company. The character of your organization is too important. Know what you stand for. (The adage is true: A person who stands for nothing falls for anything.) Set values high. Live them. See their roots go deep as they're tested, much in the way a great oak tree grows more resilient by withstanding harsh winds and storms.

If you focus appropriately on values in your corporate life, you will develop the confidence that when problems arise, when fast decisions need to be made, when temptations lurk, your gyroscope is set. You'll weather the elements. You'll be able to confidently say, "We've mastered this particular Monday!"

11

People First

Never be sympathetic with the soul whose case

makes you come to the conclusion that God is hard.

God is more tender than we can conceive.

OSWALD CHAMBERS

Attending Billy Graham's crusade in New York City in June 2005 was a poignant, precious experience. Dr. Graham, age eighty-six, spoke with the same sincerity, simplicity and clarity that have marked his ministry for over fifty years. I found myself listening intently to every word.

It was Youth Night, and I was flanked by thousands of young people. They seemed to fully represent the incredible cross-section of races and national origins only New York City can produce.

Toward the end of his address, Dr. Graham leaned forward on the podium, fixed his eyes on the young people and declared with great deliberation, "God—loves—you."

If indeed this was, as many expect, Billy Graham's final crusade, he could not have deposited with his listeners a more desperately needed legacy than the message capsulated in those three words.

God loves you.

I trust these words burned in the hearts of those who heard them—as they did in mine. It is because of the Father's great love for each person that every follower of Christ is called on to put people first. Yes, many forces militate against this priority in the business world: tradeoffs with profits, dealing with underperformers, interpersonal problems. Yet from God's perspective there is no higher priority on this earth than people.

In this chapter I will expand on this theme. We begin with Megan's story, an account describing one of the most remarkable events I've ever experienced in the workplace, or anywhere.

MEGAN'S STORY

Vic had recently been appointed as our plant superintendent, and I dropped by his office to chat and see how he was getting along. His broad smile and upbeat attitude confirmed his enthusiasm for his new position. That's why it was all the more disconcerting when he stopped by my office later that same day. Gone was the smile. His grim expression belied an obviously heavy heart.

"One of our employees, a young lady, asked to see me," Vic said in a somber voice. "She requested a day off for personal reasons. Without probing, I told her that would be fine. But then she lingered as if there were something more she wanted to say." Vic paused and shook his head, "Mr. Beckett, she told me she needed the time off to have an abortion."

Vic was getting choked up. "I tried to talk to her, to tell her the company would do all it could to help. But she said she had no choice. Her mind was made up."

"Vic," I said, "I'm not sure what we ought to do. But why don't we take some time now to pray about it?"

Vic agreed, but added that he couldn't give me her name. He had pledged to keep it confidential.

At home that evening I explained the situation to Wendy. We, too, prayed for this young woman, unknown to us but known to God.

It's not completely unusual for me to wake up in the middle of the night. (Usually I can chalk it up to having had too much to eat.) But that night was different. I awoke around 2 a.m. with our employee on my mind. Suddenly—to my amazement—I "saw" her face and knew her name. Could I be dreaming? No. I was wide awake.

The next morning, still processing this unusual experience, I sought out Vic first thing. "I realize you can't tell me who spoke with you. But if I were to tell you her name, could you confirm it?" I asked.

"Yes, I guess so . . . "

"Well, it was Megan, wasn't it?"

Vic was shocked. "Of all our employees, how did you know?"

I told Vic what had happened the night before. We sat for a while in stunned silence and then agreed to have Megan join us.

"Megan, I want to say first that Vic didn't break his confidentiality with you. He never mentioned you by name. But he told me about the situation." Megan's eyes got wider, wondering what was coming next.

"Vic and I prayed about this yesterday, asking that the Lord would help us know what to do in this situation. Then last evening my wife and I prayed about it. Can you believe that during the night I woke up and *your* face and *your* name were right there in front of me? I *knew* it was you! This morning I told Vic about what happened, and he was as surprised as I am. Now I need to ask you a question, Megan. What do you think this means?"

She shifted nervously in her chair. Then she answered, "I think God must be trying to tell me something."

"That's the way I see it," I said.

As we continued talking, the tears began to flow. Megan opened up her difficult world—financial hardship, drug-related concerns with the father of her unborn child. "I just don't know how to cope. I don't see how I can make it. It's not what I want, but I don't think I have a choice . . ."

I asked Megan if we could pray together, and she said, "Yes, that would help."

"Lord," I prayed, "You must love Megan a lot. She's facing this huge decision. Would you help her know the right thing to do?"

When Megan left my office that day, neither Vic nor I had any idea what her next steps would be. Against every natural instinct to do otherwise, it seemed as though she had steeled herself for what she described as the most difficult decision in her life.

Would Megan show up to work the next day? If not, she would be following through on her decision to have an abortion. When I came into work the following morning, it was the first question I asked Vic.

"She's here," Vic said with guarded optimism. "I hope this means she's changed her mind."

"Let's speak with her," I said.

As Megan walked into my office, she looked as though a thousand-pound weight had been lifted from her shoulders.

With tears streaming down her face and an ear-to-ear smile, she burst out: "I've decided to keep my baby!"

I cried. Vic cried too. We laughed. We hugged. We assured Megan of our intention to stand with her in whatever she needed—help with medical expenses, time off, needs for the new baby—whatever. We would see that she got that assistance.

Then I sensed the Holy Spirit "tugging my sleeve." My next words were not premeditated, but came spontaneously. "Megan, you've seen how much the Lord loves you and cares for you. Would you like to invite him into your life?"

It was almost as though she was prepared for that question. Without hesitation she said, "Yes, I would." We talked briefly about what it means for a person to come to Christ, and then the three of us prayed. I'll never forget her countenance as she opened her eyes and looked up. In those brief moments, Megan had been transformed into a new person.

Even now, I can't find adequate words to describe how much this experience meant to me. To see the Lord's enormous care for that young lady in trouble. To witness the miracle of God revealing her identity to me in the middle of the night. And above all, to see this take place in a normal manufacturing company with "ordinary" people like Vic and me. Two lives saved—Megan's unborn child and, spiritually, Megan herself. What an awesome privilege!

GOD'S HEART TOWARD PEOPLE

In earlier chapters, I have referred to the modern phenomenon of God's activity in the workplace. The scope and breadth of what is happening encompasses many thousands of organizations, large and small. It's not an illusion. It's not a passing fad. It's real.

But *why* is it happening? Of the many reasons we could cite, I believe the most important is God's passionate desire to reach and develop people. He is focusing on the workplace because that's where the people are, worldwide, by the hundreds of millions. Most of these people do not attend church. They don't go to evangelistic meetings. They may catch a religious TV broadcast now and then, or pick up a helpful book. But one thing we know: they do go to work, for over two thousand hours each year.

Would Megan have taken her problem to a pastor if she'd had one? Possibly. Would she have sought out expensive counseling? Unlikely. Yet in the middle of her workday, God arranged for the most important event of her life. How vitally important that those whom God has sent into the world's workplaces do all they can to align with God's priority to help people.

The Bible is rich in references to God's love toward us. David speaks of "saints . . . in whom is *all* [the Lord's] delight" (Psalm 16:3, italics added). "All" simply could not be more comprehensive. The prophet Zephaniah assures us,

> The LORD your God is with you,
>> he is mighty to save.
> He will take great delight in you,
>> he will quiet you with his love,
>> he will rejoice over you with singing. (Zephaniah 3:17)

What a beautiful picture—the Lord himself delighting in us, even singing in joy over his people.

Jesus echoed this aspect of God's nature, for better than anyone else, he knew his Father's heart. On one occasion he told the story of a prodigal son. You'll recall that the younger of two brothers had asked for his share of his father's inheritance, left home and squandered it in profligate living. After hitting bottom, he eventually returned, hoping at minimum to live as one of his father's hired hands. Instead, his father "killed the fattened calf" in celebration, provoking intense jealousy in the older brother.

A GREAT WAY OFF

For the moment, I'd like to focus not on the son but on the father. "But when [the errant son] was still *a great way off*, his father saw him and had compassion, and ran and fell on his neck and kissed him" (Luke 15:20 NKJV, italics added).

As I read this account, I am impressed that it was not by accident that the father saw the son when he was "a great way off." (Does God the Father not look longingly for each of *us* when we're a long way off?) I imagine that many times each day following his son's departure, the father had gazed down the long, dusty road with misty eyes, hoping beyond hope that perhaps—just perhaps—this would be the day his son would return. Now months had passed. Would this day be any different?

As the hot morning sun rose in the eastern sky, the father occasionally glanced down the road as he went about his work. Then, to his surprise, he spotted a lone figure dimly silhouetted against the horizon. For a moment his heart leapt, but just as quickly stilled. It was just another traveler; perhaps a random visitor. But then a surge of hope coursed through his tired soul. There was something familiar in the frame, the gait of this person. Could it be his son?

His eyes strained as the figure drew closer. Yes! This *was* his son! Whatever the sorrow, whatever the pain from the past, there was at that moment one overwhelming emotion. With a depth of compassion only love can understand, the father hurled his now-energized body down the road toward the one he longed for, his arms open wide. With great sobs, the father "fell on his neck and kissed him." His son, once dead, had come back to life. His son, once lost, had been found.

In telling this story, I believe Jesus wanted his listeners to understand the heart of his own Father. He was saying, "Don't you see how much my Dad loves you? What you've done isn't the issue. No sin is too great. He yearns for you to come home; he longs to restore you to himself." How many prodigal sons and daughters are there in your work world and mine? How often have I looked on their troubled past, their poor performance, their unkempt appearance . . . and callously hit the minimize button? Should I not instead view them through the Father's eyes, and with nothing less than profound compassion?

WORKPLACE DIFFICULTIES

While we can, and should, view each person in the workplace with compassion, practical issues remain: poor habits, substandard performance, bad attitudes and unsuitability for a particular job. I find these issues are commonly on the minds of businesspeople. They want to know how to deal with them and whether they can be resolved redemptively.

In my view we should make every reasonable effort to help people work through their difficulties, going the extra mile to turn failure into success. Sometimes problems are those of timing. Megan didn't come to a place of coping with her unplanned pregnancy until her personal crisis was fully formed. The prodigal son didn't head home until his stomach gnawed with hunger. It is tremendously satisfying when a struggling employee is able to see the difficulty and make needed adjustments. But there are times when even our best efforts are insufficient. Then it may be necessary to take the toughest step of all: termination. However, when it's done with compassion and grace, the outcome can be redemptive.

This was brought home to me in an unusual (and humorous) way. Of all settings, I was in a dental chair being prepped for the replacement of a filling. Just as my mouth was full of dental hardware so I could only mumble, the dental technician said, out of the blue, "You're Mr. Beckett, aren't you?"

I grunted assent.

"Well, I want to thank you for firing my husband."

I was stuck. I couldn't move. I couldn't speak. I could only listen to the ensuing monologue.

"It happened ten years ago," she said. "A few days after your company hired my husband, he was notified he had failed a drug test." (Later, we changed our policy. We now wait for testing results before a person begins work.) "You may not recall," she continued, "but you called him into your office before he left. You said, 'You realize I don't have any choice but to terminate you. But I want to tell you something. You're at a crossroads. You can keep going the way you are, and the results are very predictable. Or you can take this as a wake-up call. You can decide you're going to turn your life around.'"

I'm sure the technician couldn't see the beads of perspiration on my forehead under all the paraphernalia as she continued: "I want you to know, my husband took your advice. Today, he's a good father, a good husband, and he has a fine job. Thank you for firing my husband!"

I wish I could say that all our terminations have turned out this way. They haven't. With some, there has been lingering resentment and a sense of injustice. But I am grateful that many have "made lemonade" out of the lemons, moving on to productive and rewarding work careers. Regardless of the outcome, however, we must be prepared to take action when a situation can't be brought around. In a strange way, it's an aspect of our care for people.

PEOPLE VERSUS PROFITS

Workplace difficulties frequently appear when decisions pit people against profits. Nathan Sanders, a pastor and counselor to business people in Federalsburg, Maryland, asked: "Should a business owner pay more attention to the welfare of his employees or to profitability?" This is a tough question, with many nuances, and many practical implications. But from a biblical perspective, we're never wrong to put people before profits. Ultimately people produce profits, and without people there would *be* no profits, not even a business. The right people, properly placed, respected and rewarded, are the single greatest key to increasing business and profitability. This is what Jim Collins means by "getting the right people on the bus."

But Collins also says we've got to get the wrong people off the bus. He cites a Wells Fargo executive's view on this difficult issue: "The only way to deliver to the people who are achieving is to not burden them with the people who are not achieving" (*Good to Great,* p. 53). We make every effort to help people work through difficulties, often with good results. Be we've also erred in having the "second mile" become the third, forth and fifth, putting off the inevitable termination. Of course that final step, when other options are exhausted, should be taken with compassion, but it must be taken. The price is simply too great otherwise.

I know of no business today that can survive while failing to improve productivity, use its resources more wisely and employ its people more creatively. Global competition is too intense. We tell our employees that we need to "continually earn the right to manufacture in Northern Ohio." Complacency is not an option. We must steadily improve what we're doing if we're going to stay viable.

OUTSOURCING

The contentious topic of outsourcing is too vast to adequately cover here, but I'd like to offer a few thoughts relating to people. Shipping jobs overseas has been wrenching for many, especially in the manufacturing sector. Yet this same shift is estimated to have saved U.S. consumers roughly $600 billion since the mid-1990s (*Fortune* magazine, October 4, 2004). What is the "higher good," especially when we consider the benefit to foreign workers, who, perhaps for the first time, are enjoying opportunities to earn a good income, provide for their families and even own their own homes? While many would argue otherwise, I believe outsourcing may be a case where short-term loss to some will, longer-term, be more than offset by gains to others worldwide, and ultimately to our own country.

Another consideration: Thomas L. Friedman, in his insightful book *The World Is Flat,* says, "Most companies build offshore factories not simply to obtain cheaper labor for products they want to sell in America or Europe. Another motivation is to serve that foreign market" (p. 123). In fact, he notes that the U.S. Commerce Department finds that 90 percent of the output from U.S.-owned offshore factories is sold to foreign customers.

This is actually our motivation with one of our companies as we open a manufacturing facility in China. The products we make there will be used in Asia rather than shipped back to the United States. China itself is a vast, rapidly growing market with over one billion potential customers, an opportunity too great to be ignored. In addition to the jobs we create, we want to "export" what we've learned about building a business that honors God. We want a company in mainland China where each person is deeply respected, where core values and high ethical standards are nonnegotiable and excellence in quality and every aspect of performance is the norm. It will be a challenge, we know, in a country where the prevailing culture is so different from our own. But we believe God wants to extend his kingdom not just into China but into workplaces around the world, helping enable and ennoble the lives of those who are often in greatest need, physically, economically and spiritually.

GUIDING PRINCIPLES

As we confront the challenges surrounding the employment of people, companies can help themselves enormously by establishing and communicating governing philosophies and guidelines.

Though I had hoped to find otherwise, relatively few of the many organizations whose core philosophies I reviewed focus specifically on the *intrinsic worth* of the individual.

Here are a few statements from those companies that *do* reflect an underlying respect for people:

- Alaska Airlines: "Caring about and helping people is the soul of Alaska Airlines. We believe our lives are enriched by individual acts of kindness and compassion."

- Conoco: "At Conoco, we strive to create an inclusive work environment that treats all people with dignity and respect, and encourages employees to express their ideas and develop to their maximum ability."

- Lanier: "We will treat all people—within our company and without—in a fair, courteous and dignified manner to promote mutual respect and demonstrate our commitment to equality, justice and the family."

- Metokote: "Our people are our source of strength. They provide our corporate intelligence and determine our reputation and vitality. Employee involvement and teamwork are the core fiber of this primary resource."

In our company, as noted earlier, one of our core values states our expectation that each employee is to have "a profound respect for the individual," whether that person is a fellow employee, a supplier, a customer, or a member of the community. We then expand on our expectations regarding our work environment as follows:

- We want our work and work relationships to be dynamic, challenging, rewarding and respectful—and all employees to be knowledgeable and well trained, with a strong sense of accountability and personal responsibility.

- We anticipate ongoing change, and want change to be viewed as an opportunity, not a threat.

- We expect individual growth, and will encourage such growth by providing easily available opportunities for education and training.

- We will foster a culture of innovation throughout the company encouraging both large and many small improvements.

- We want to build on the concept of teams and teamwork, encouraging good communications, mutual support and respect for our fellow employees regardless of position.

These guidelines are beacons pointing toward a work environment that encourages our people to flourish in their work and have an integral role in our company's success. We consider these principles the practical outworking of an underlying reality: God cares deeply for people.

A CEO WITH A HEART FOR PEOPLE

During the Reagan administration I was privileged to make several visits to the White House. On a few occasions I was part of small groups who met with the president. Mr. Reagan always struck me as a person who had a genuine interest in others. In fact, one time I was with about twenty guests and watched in amazement as the president made his way around our conference table and warmly greeted each by name.

On one of my visits to the White House, I was with a large

group touring this elegant building dating back to the early 1800s. I had been through the White House before and was a little ahead of the rest of the group. When I arrived at the final room on our tour, the only other person in it was an imposing Secret Service agent. As I walked over to greet him, I noticed a large painting of President Reagan nearby. Instead of my customary "hello," I pointed to the portrait and said, more brashly than usual, "What do you think of this guy?"

"We love him!" It was not what I expected to hear, especially from this tall, muscular guardian of the president.

"What do you mean, 'We love him?'" I asked back.

"Look," he said, " I've worked for seven of them." (My mind did a fast rewind to the immediate predecessors: Carter, Ford, Nixon, Johnson, Kennedy and Eisenhower. He had worked for *all* of them.)

The agent continued, "I've seen him in good times and bad, even at 2 a.m. on Air Force One when he's dog tired. He's always the same. He's interested in us. He wants to know how we're doing. He asks about our families. We love him!"

This testimony "from the trenches" spoke volumes to me about this CEO. In the midst of his myriad responsibilities, he was interested in the "little guy"—who, in his estimation, was not little at all. The president of the United States had an intrinsic and profound respect for every person. He had a heart that reflected that of the heavenly Father, for God cares deeply for people. So must we.

12

Stewardship

Try not to become a man of success, but a man of value.

In 1979 the Middle East oil embargo sent our company into a tail-spin. Triggered by the overthrow of the Shah of Iran, the embargo forced the price of oil sky-high. In a very short time the market for our products was slashed by half. Everyone felt the impact. Refueling cars meant waiting in long lines at gas pumps. Higher fuel prices created inflationary ripples through the entire economy. The national "misery index"—the sum of unemployment and inflation—hit a peak of 22 percent in June 1980. Unemployment in our small Ohio community soared past 30 percent.

The product manufactured by our company uses heating oil to heat homes. In 1980 there were some 12.5 million oil-heated dwelling units in North America. Consequently increased oil prices meant an added burden of over $7 billion to residential fuel bills. So when an inventor came to us with a new technology to improve fuel burning, he had our undivided attention.

While the technology seemed sound, the price tag for adopting it was high, especially in light of our deteriorating market. I was at a point in my spiritual growth where I had become more confident the Lord would direct us if we would ask him for guidance. And guide us he did. The direction I sought came as I was reading the account of Jesus feeding a multitude of people. Yet it came not from the miracle itself when the loaves and fishes were multiplied but in what happened afterward: "When they had all had enough to eat, he said to his disciples, 'Gather the pieces that are left over. *Let nothing be wasted*'" (John 6:12, italics added).

How amazing! I thought. *Five thousand people are sitting there, well fed, basking in the afterglow of a feast that began with five small barley loaves and two small fishes. Yet here is the miracle-worker turned steward.* Jesus was paying attention to the leftovers, making it his priority to conserve a resource his Father had provided.

Then it struck me. Would Jesus not likewise want our company—the nation's leading producer of heating oil burners—to help our customers save fuel *and* conserve the world's oil reserves? Had that oil not been carefully formed and stored, a "miracle" in its own way?

This flash of insight became my wake-up call to the Lord's perspective on practical stewardship in our company. With newfound conviction, we invested in the new technology and began a five-year program to bring it to market.

Ironically, we were never able to commercialize this combustion concept. In its final configuration it was just too complex and too costly for our market. Yet there was a silver lining. Conservation became a way of life for us. Since the time of that decision we've been aggressive in energy management and waste elimination wherever possible, including the pursuit of "lean manufacturing" approaches throughout our operations. Significantly, we have leveraged other improvements in combustion technology, helping homeowners to decrease their use of oil by two *billion* gallons in the last several decades. That amount of oil would fill a line of railroad tank cars long enough to circle the globe!

STEWARDSHIP: MORE THAN MONEY

Recently I was asked how I would define stewardship. My answer to that question has changed over the years. Early on I associated stewardship mostly with money, as with the annual "stewardship campaign" in our church to meet the coming year's budget. Now I define it much more broadly: caring for resources that are not our own. Our company's Guiding Principles declare that we are committed "to be wise and able stewards of the trust he [God] has placed with us."

Webster's definition for *steward* focuses on the idea of household management: "A person put in charge of the affairs of a large household or estate, whose duties include supervision of the kitchen and the servants, management of household accounts, etc." That concept is readily expandable to such "large households" as the modern business where people in every role can have an influence on how wisely or unwisely resources are managed:

- The janitor, as he or she manages cleaning supplies
- The supervisor, helping his work crew be most efficient (time is an incredibly valuable resource)
- The engineer, looking for ways to eliminate unneeded complexity in product design

- The salesperson, deciding on how much to spend on lodging and meals, and what items should and shouldn't go into the expense account

- The CEO, in optimizing overall use of the company's capital, staffing and marketplace opportunities

Stewardship as a recurrent theme in the Bible has close ties to the workplace. The concept originates in the Garden. Adam is set in charge of managing God's creation (Genesis 2:15). The Garden, Adam and everything else belonged to the Lord.

The psalmist declares the totality of God's ownership:

The earth is the LORD's, and everything in it,
the world, and all who live in it. (Psalm 24:1)

What is omitted? Nothing. The molecule, the mouse, the flower's fragrance, the sapphire's sparkle—all belong to the Lord.

In the New Testament, Jesus uses several illustrations involving stewardship. In one, he tells of a wasteful steward who consequently loses his job: "There was a rich man whose manager was accused of wasting his possessions" (Luke 16:1). The point of the parable? "Whoever can be trusted with very little can also be trusted with much, and whoever is dishonest with very little will also be dishonest with much. So if you have not been trustworthy in handling worldly wealth, who will trust you with true riches? And if you have not been trustworthy with someone else's property, who will give you property of your own?" (Luke 16:10-12).

I recall a story told to me by an elderly neighbor, Mr. Bado. As a young lad growing up in Hungary, Bado was made a houseboy in the home of a wealthy family. As he went about his cleaning chores, which included straightening cushions on the chairs and sofas, he would find coins that had apparently slipped from people's pockets. Without fail, he would take them to the owner. After a month or so, young Mr. Bado noticed he was not finding any more coins. Without a word being spoken, the realization hit him. The coins had been placed there intentionally. He was being tested in small things. The owner now knew his houseboy could be trusted in the larger affairs of his household. Years later Mr. Bado moved to the "new country" (as he called the United States), where he opened a garden center. He soon established a reputation for integrity, and his business prospered through the end of his humble but exemplary life. He was able to be trusted with much.

Expanding the scope of this topic, Jesus applied the concept of stewardship in a surprising way, namely the degree of preparedness of a person for his return: "It will be good for those servants whose master finds them watching when he comes" (Luke 12:37). The person who was not a good steward in this illustration was preoccupied, unprepared. But the "faithful and wise steward" was attentive, watchful. That was his stewardship responsibility. (Note that it had nothing to do with money.)

THE EARLY CHURCH'S VIEW ON STEWARDSHIP

The apostle Paul had a broad view of stewardship. For example, he refers to himself and his companions in ministry as "servants of Christ and stewards of the mysteries of God" (1 Corinthians 4:1 NKJV; see also Colossians 1:25-29; Ephesians 3:2-10). He understood that he had been entrusted with insights concerning God and his kingdom. Being a good steward demanded that he give his full energy—even his life, if necessary—to sharing with others what he had been given. The issue was faithfulness. "Moreover it is required in stewards that one be found faithful" (1 Corinthians 4:2 NKJV). Paul knew he would account for the trust he had been given.

Paul considered an elder (one with leadership responsibility in the church) as a "steward of God" (Titus 1:7 NKJV). That meant being a good trustee for God in every aspect—his kingdom, his creation, his character, his ways, his standards. How would you apply this concept of stewardship in your leadership responsibilities at home, at work, in your community and nation?

The apostle Peter said gifts given to individuals by the grace of God are worthy of good stewardship: "As each one has received a gift, minister it to one another, as good stewards of the manifold grace of God" (1 Peter 4:10 NKJV). Gifts to be ministered included prayer, care for others, extending love, hospitality and serving (see 1 Peter 4:7-11). God gives us gifts not for our own use but for the benefit of others. The essence of good stewardship is to manage them faithfully.

In the 1981 movie *Chariots of Fire,* Scottish missionary Eric Liddell explains his passion for running to his sister, Jennie. With great conviction he says, "I believe God made me for a purpose, but he also made me fast. And when I run, I feel his pleasure." Running was his God-given gift, which he ultimately stewarded on a world stage in the 1924 Summer Olympics in Paris.

WHAT ARE WE RESPONSIBLE FOR?

Some years ago, Dr. Henry Blackaby suggested I do a "spiritual inventory." (I referred to this earlier.) By that he meant I should list areas where I had capacities, abilities and relationships that could be used to further the purposes of God. Two pages later I was still writing, amazed at how much God had placed in my care! That exercise immediately increased my sense of responsibility to properly steward what I had been given.

Here are some of the broad categories where most of us have stewardship responsibilities.

- Family
- Time
- Influence
- Knowledge, understanding and wisdom
- Resources
- Abilities
- Relationships with God and with others
- Work
- The spiritual atmosphere around (over) us

To comment on a just a few, let's focus on family, influence, resources and spiritual atmosphere:

Family. A challenge for all of us is to balance work and family. That challenge has intensified in recent years. Not only have work demands increased (especially with the relentless squeeze on profit margins and corporate downsizing), but also spouses and children have greater commitments and involvements. It is difficult even to find time to be together. I don't come with all the answers but rather with a brief testimony to God's faithfulness. We had many hurdles to overcome raising our six children. There were times when I wondered if they—and I—would make it. Now all are grown, finished with college and involved in significant work. We've been blessed with wonderful sons- and daughters-in-law and grandchildren.

During the years our children were at home, we tried to make them a top priority, even though it was difficult. We focused on three primary areas: love, discipline and fun. I'm grateful that Wendy was able to be at home, providing motherly care and earnest prayer. Our children knew they were deeply loved and appreciated. Though they had lots of squabbles growing up, they are now close friends, and I am working directly with two sons and a son-in-law. Today we can look back and see tremendous fruit from our investment in family. I'm so glad God helped us take this stewardship responsibility so seriously.

Influence. Each of us has a sphere of responsibility where we have maximum influence. For all his far-ranging travels and activities, the apostle Paul sought to stay "within the limits of the sphere which God appointed" (2 Corinthians 10:13 NKJV). Within God's prescribed limits we can operate effectively. Outside those limits, we don't. (It's sort of like staying under your umbrella when it's raining.) Knowing our limits makes it easier to say no to activities outside our boundaries.

I keep this pungent little reminder in view in my office:

In Praise of No

No may be the most efficient time saver in the English language. What it lacks in grace is more than offset by its brevity. You don't equivocate when you say *No*, though you may risk offense. Used with discretion and appropriate garnishes, *No* can save you hours of time. *No* returns responsibility to its rightful owner. *No* enables you to focus on your priorities. *No* protects you from your own good heart. Do not scorn the pungent clarity of *No*. It can be your ticket to success.

How do we best steward the influence we have been given? It's important for us to answer that question correctly. You may recall (from chapter seven) those in Babylon who were judged for using their influence improperly—"great men" who led entire nations astray. The larger our sphere, the greater our responsibility. Jesus said, "From everyone who has been given much shall much be required" (Luke 12:48 NASB).

Resources. How are we managing the resources entrusted to us? In the account of the poor widow, Jesus stressed how vital it is that our hearts be right in managing wealth, regardless of whether we have much or little (see Luke 21:3). In fact, small gifts with good motives can multiply in surprising ways.

I saw this principle at work some years ago when a godly widow in England gave a gift of $1,000 toward the start-up of a Christian college in New York City. Compared to the millions needed to launch the new school, hers was truly a "widow's mite." Yet God used her modest contribution in an amazing way. Someone who heard about it redirected $3.5 million to the college—funds which had originally been designated for another use. This in turn triggered other gifts such that, as of this writing, that initial gift has multiplied thirty-five thousand times to over $35 million—all from a very small beginning. We have stewardship responsibility for resources entrusted to us—whether a mite or a million.

I gleaned views on stewarding resources from the purpose statements of several large companies: W. C. Bradley Co. states as a core value "stewardship of what has been entrusted to us in serving others." First Southern National Bank intends to be "responsible stewards of those resources entrusted to us." And Lanier Worldwide, a division of Harris, views the resources in their care as a "sacred trust."

Whether for an individual or an organization, resources are indeed a trust to be stewarded with diligence and discipline.

Spiritual atmosphere. One of the areas we must steward is the spiritual atmosphere around (and over) us. As strange as it may seem, through prayer and intercession we can actually influence the spiritual climate surrounding our families, work and communities.

The apostle Paul informed us that we have a fight on our hands. "[We battle] against the spiritual forces of evil in the heavenly realms" (Ephesians 6:10-12). We take this fight on through prayer. It wasn't just theory for the great apostle. In spite of the enormous obstacles he faced, he prevailed throughout the entire province of Asia (see Acts 19:20, 26). Think of this. One man, faithful to his calling, working within his sphere, transformed the culture of an entire continent! Paul made a difference—and you can too.

HOW DOES A STEWARD FUNCTION?

We need to keep in mind that the steward is not necessarily the boss or the owner. He is one under authority, serving at the pleasure of another. He does not call the shots. His obligation is to be attentive, committed, willing and obedient. Our stewardship is to our heavenly Father. We represent him and his kingdom here on earth.

In closing this chapter I want to share some brief thoughts on what faithful stewardship looks like in the following areas:

- Perseverance

- Generosity

- Guardianship

- Understanding "success"

Perseverance. The Christian life is not easy. (For that matter, neither is the non-Christian life.) The book of Acts and Paul's letters make it clear that opposition is a consistent fact of life. The apostle cited this as a proof of his authenticity "in great endurance; in troubles, hardships and distresses" (2 Corinthians 6:4).

Compared with some of my friends, my life has been remarkably easy. (I've occasionally wondered if that's an indication I may not have pressed in hard enough.) Yet there have been times when both our family and business have had to persevere through difficult times: accidents, illness, deaths, fires, misunderstandings and ruptured relationships. Through these situations we've had to persevere. We could not give up. Eventually we were able to see that God had a purpose, even in the greatest difficulties. But only in facing and going through them were we able to see his larger design.

Generosity. Earlier, we observed that stewardship is much broader than handling money. How we handle our finances is not only important for its own sake—it is a reflection of where our hearts are. The late Larry Burkett, a pioneer in the area of financial responsibility, cataloged over two thousand references in the Bible related to money and economics. This subject is indeed high on the Lord's agenda for us.

Two quick thoughts for our purposes here. First, the foundation of all financial stewardship is a simple realization: it all belongs to the Lord. It's his, not ours. It's on loan to us. God owns "the cattle on a thousand hills" (Psalm 50:10), and as somebody once added, "Guess what? He owns the hills, too!" When we give, we're basically redirecting what has been given to us, whether we have earned it or inherited it.

Second, God loves generosity. In fact, he throws down the gauntlet before us. How about this challenge? "'Bring the whole tithe into the storehouse. . . . Test me in this,' says the LORD Almighty, 'and see if I will not throw open the floodgates of heaven and pour out so much blessing that you will not have room enough for it'" (Malachi 3:10). Jesus likewise encourages abundant generosity: "Give, and it will be given to you. A good measure, pressed down, shaken together and running over" (Luke 6:38).

When I say God loves generosity in his servants, I'm not talking about something I just read in a book. Beginning with a decision Wendy and I made years ago to tithe (give at least 10 percent of our income), we have seen his provision for us increase steadily, and with it our capacity to give more. It is one of our greatest joys to hear from the Lord and then give as he directs.

Guardianship. A true steward stands firm when the going gets tough. Jesus made a distinction between the shepherd and the hireling: "The hired hand is not the shepherd who owns the sheep. So when he sees the wolf coming, he abandons the sheep and runs away" (John 10:12). There have been times in my business career when I would have given anything for a one-way ticket to a fishing lodge, at least for a few days.

One of those occasions was the time, mentioned earlier, when a labor organization was seeking to unionize our employees. In the middle of that difficult encounter, reality set in. I was not a "hireling." As the leader of my company, I did not have the option to cut and run. I had to stick it out and see it through to its conclusion. So I became a tenacious steward on behalf of those who did not want to be unionized. I believe this was a major factor in our employees' decision to remain independent of the union.

Jesus has given us a sacred trust. He has handed us the stewardship of his kingdom on earth. And he fully expects us to jealously guard all he has placed in our care.

Understanding "success." Some people "fail to succeed." Lloyd Pedersen from Michigan has been in business thirty-five years. He writes, "Some day I am going to write a book called, 'Chronicles of a Failure.' It will appeal to the majority of men in the world who never achieve significant business success—who don't quite live up to their expectations of life, even though many have had tremendous success in raising families and in effective ministry." That book is desperately needed.

The dominant driving force in the work world is "success." We passionately pursue it yet think little about what success really is. The goal is so elusive that sometimes we achieve it without realizing it. Or we change the target of our success and live in a state of discontent. Few words in the English language are as difficult to define. There ought to be some good "measuring stick." But there isn't.

Webster's Dictionary defines *success* as "a favorable or satisfactory outcome or result," a meaning which is anything but precise. The word *success* is hardly mentioned in the Scriptures (although the word *prosper* is used in older translations and translated "success" in newer versions). Among the few examples: on entering the Promised Land, God told Joshua he would be *successful* if he carefully obeyed the law passed on to him by Moses (Joshua 1:7-8). Hezekiah, one of Israel's few good kings, had *success* in whatever he undertook because "the LORD was with him" (2 Kings 18:7). Nehemiah prayed for *success* as he brought his petition to rebuild Jerusalem to the king he served (Nehemiah 1:11).

J. R. Miller, an American Presbyterian minister at the turn of the twentieth century, says: "Christ is building his kingdom with the broken things of earth. People desire only the strong, successful, victorious and unbroken things in life to build their kingdoms, but God is the God of the unsuccessful—the God of those who have failed. He can lift earth's saddest failure up to heaven's glory" (in *Streams in the Desert*).

I have no illusions. Neither this, nor a hundred books will alter the prevailing mindset of what constitutes success. But my appeal to my colleagues in the marketplace who desire to follow Christ is to focus on a biblical term close to God's heart. The word is *faithful*. And it is intimately linked with good stewardship.

While *success* is used infrequently in the Scriptures, the word *faithful* is used throughout. Here are a few examples from Proverbs to Revelation (all italics added):

- A *faithful* man will be richly blessed. (Proverbs 28:20)

- Well done, good and *faithful* servant! (Matthew 25:21)

- Those who have been given a trust must prove *faithful*. (1 Corinthians 4:2)

- [The apostle Paul wrote] to the holy and *faithful* brothers in Christ. (Colossians 1:2)

- The Lamb will overcome them because he is Lord of lords and King of kings—and with him will be his called, chosen and *faithful* followers. (Revelation 17:14)

I once heard these words from a politician who was running for office against overwhelming odds: "God hasn't called me to be successful. He's called me to be faithful." That mindset may not have gotten him elected, but it freed him to focus on what was most important to him, regardless of the outcome.

Earlier I told the story of the extraordinary time Wendy and I had with businesspeople in eastern Russia. Not surprisingly, in that country so long deprived of opportunity there is a huge hunger for "success." In trying to communicate an understanding of success to them I said, "There are many measures, not all of them good or reliable. But success is not always what you assume it to be." Then I pulled two photographs from my Bible. (I keep them there, where they accompany me on my travels.) One was of Wendy and me. "Success for me has been the joy of a wonderful marriage to the same woman for over forty years." The next photo I pulled out was of our extended family, including children-in-law and grandchildren—over twenty people in one picture. "These pictures," I said, "represent a far greater measure of success for me than all I have achieved in business, all I have earned, all the recognition I've received."

Suddenly, led by the women in the audience, the room erupted in applause. Those photos made them understand: true success reaches far beyond monetary gain and momentary fame.

Stewardship touches every area of life. How we manage time, family, friendships, responsibilities, our spiritual growth and even success reflects our attitude toward God and our relationship with him. He is carefully assessing how we steward what is entrusted to us, holding in reserve words he eventually longs to bestow on his followers: "Well done, good and faithful servant!" (Matthew 25:23). May we conduct our lives mindful of the sacred trust we've been given, making it our deepest desire to receive from our Lord this ultimate commendation.

13

Serving

Serve wholeheartedly.

EPHESIANS 6:7

Suppose you were asked to turn around a large division of a multibillion dollar publicly traded company? The division was on financial "life-support," losing money, consuming large amounts of capital and experiencing negative cash flow. Fast action would be necessary. This was the business environment John Aden inherited as he walked into the top job at the Mac Tools division of The Stanley Works in June 2000. Not only was John new to the automotive tools industry, but this was also his first stint as a corporate president. And he was only thirty-three years old!

As bad as the financials were, the nonfinancial aspects of the company were even worse. "There was a problem under every stone I turned over," John said during our interview. "We discovered fraud in one of our units. People were stealing in others. The company's culture was driven by greed, pride and fear. Expenses had spun out of control. It was not a pretty picture." A once-proud and prosperous company serving over 600,000 customers through 1,500 distributors had fallen into disrepair.

You may think this story is an improbable introduction to a chapter on serving. But serving is much more than the job of the factory janitor, the retail merchant's restocking clerk or the airline's baggage handler. There's a side to serving we don't usually see: service from the top down. The question on John Aden's mind as he took the reins was: "How could I, as a very young president, *serve* Mac Tools, yet take the tough action that would be required?" As we'll see, Aden served Mac Tools in ways that, just a few years after his arrival, produced some stunning results. But these did not come without radical and painful steps. He began by thinking through what service really is.

"I realized that for many, 'serving' and 'servant leadership' had become buzzwords, made popular by business authors and leadership consultants. But I saw some troubling aspects to what they were saying," says Aden. "They view 'serving' as the next level on a leadership continuum—another resource in the manager's toolkit. But I believe this approach can become just another way of controlling, or even manipulating others, say for improved performance or productivity. It amounts to 'service . . . so that . . . ' rather than service for its own sake."

John has continued to grow in his understanding of what real service means. "Service that is selfish is far from the biblical concept. Biblical service doesn't waiver, whether times are good or bad. Biblical service doesn't change based on how people are performing. Biblical service is an unshakable attitude that puts others first." It was *this* kind of service that energized John Aden to take on a near-impossible challenge at Mac Tools.

TACKLING THE TASK

Aden began his difficult task with some intense surveillance. (Remember how Nehemiah's first step after arriving in Jerusalem was to inspect the city's broken walls?) "The first thing I did was to get out in the field. I spent 90 of my first 110 days out of the office. I spent at least an hour with all 120 district managers. I spent twelve days riding on distributors' trucks. I held roundtables everywhere I went—listening and gathering data."

When Aden reviewed all he had gleaned, he realized there was "a huge gap between what my direct reports were telling me and what was really happening in our business. I realized we had totally lost connectivity with our customers." The situation was so dire that John felt he had no choice but to remove six of seven regional managers and replace them with people he could depend on.

"This was the beginning of two years of really hard change. We also had to radically adjust the compensation model for about 1,000 of our distributors. The net result was a 20-30 percent pay cut across the board. People were angry . . . in fact, *so* angry I was receiving personal threats." But there was no choice, and the huge restructuring continued. "By the end of the first year, fourteen of my fifteen direct reports had been replaced, and within two years, well over 100 of the top 150 people in the company were new in their positions."

John now looks back on the early stages of restructuring with some lingering regrets. As necessary as the action was, it was a bruising, painful process. As a result, he became more intentional in his approach to failing employees, even to bearing some of the responsibility for their failure. "I now realize that every time a person was terminated, it was really a reflection on my leadership. It is a tough reality to face. But I think that all of us as leaders have to hold ourselves more accountable for the success of people that we lead—to do all we can to help them reach their full potential."

Things were marginally better after the first two years, but more difficult steps were necessary. "I realized we were trying to pump air into a balloon that had a hole in the other side." At that point, John became more deliberate in addressing these critical issues redemptively. "I realized we had to close a whole division and let 54 percent of our people go. I concluded that if there was a way to do this and still help people maintain their dignity, I wanted to do it. We worked out severance packages; we invested in people; we helped them land on their feet." John Aden approached this "monster change" with open communication. He knew people needed to know the truth, and though his discussions with employees were painful, they were remarkably well received. "I felt God's presence more than I ever thought possible," he said.

WHY SERVE?

We'll return to John Aden and the Mac Tool story, but first a question. Why is an attitude toward service so important to the Lord, even for the head of a big company? Here are some biblical insights:

- *God created us for service* (Genesis 2:15). Mankind's fall occurred when they set aside a serving mentality and sought to "be like God" (Genesis 3:5).

- *Satan despises serving.* He even sought equivalency with God: "I will ascend. . . . I will sit enthroned. . . . I will make myself like the Most High" (Isaiah 14:13-14).

- *Our first order of service is to God.* "Worship the Lord your God, and serve him only" (Matthew 4:10; Deuteronomy 6:13).

- *Then, we're to serve others.* "Serve one another in love" (Galatians 5:13).

- *Servanthood is voluntary.* "Choose for yourselves this day whom you will serve" (Joshua 24:15). The decision to serve resides with the person serving—unlike slavery, where a decision is imposed by another.

- *Our work can be service.* "Whatever you do, work at it with all your heart, as working for the Lord, not for men. . . . It is the Lord Christ you are serving" (Colossians 3:23-24).

- *Our capacity to serve can be developed.* Christian leaders are "to prepare God's people for works of service" (Ephesians 4:12).

Serving is integral to how God wants his kingdom on earth to function. Jesus emphasized this when he said, "You know that the rulers of the Gentiles lord it over them, and their high officials exercise authority over them. Not so with you. Instead, whoever wants to become great among you must be your servant" (Matthew 20:25-26).

While this chapter is primarily focused on how an executive can serve his or her organization, the lessons apply regardless of position. Consider a company's maintenance department, with its responsibility to keep equipment and machinery functioning properly. I've been in businesses where highly skilled maintenance people build their own little kingdoms, to be in control and indispensable. But a maintenance person with a serving mentality looks for ways to help others be effective in *their* responsibilities. They respond to problems promptly and cheerfully. They take preventive steps to avoid breakdowns. They are teachers and trainers, helping others come up the learning curve.

Supervisors, too, can serve. I've found the most effective supervisors are actually coaches, facilitators and encouragers for their people—not the much-stereotyped "straw bosses" of earlier types of leadership.

I'm sure John Aden, by exemplifying a servant's heart from his leadership position, helped enable others to find ways to serve their colleagues throughout the company.

BREAKTHROUGHS AT MAC TOOL

John's first act of service was to do everything he possibly could to make sure Mac Tool survived, and that critical goal was achieved. Compared to four years prior, the financial indicators were encouraging. Though total sales had declined by 30 percent over a three-year period due to the closing of an unprofitable division, the offsetting good news was that selling and administrative expenses were cut by 70 percent, and the company moved into the black. As Mac Tools began to generate more cash than it consumed, the problem of negative cash flow was addressed. With the capital base lowered, return on capital employed (ROCE) levels became positive and eventually exceeded the cost of capital—*very* good news.

Companies are often criticized for radical restructuring that eliminates hundreds or thousands of jobs. Many times that criticism is warranted. I'm always uncomfortable when I hear such cavalier directives such as "We need to reduce headcount by 15 percent," as though people were a commodity, like surplus inventory. But with Mac Tools the restructuring was essential. The result? The company survived to "fight another day." As with an individual suffering from a serious disease, radical surgery may be required if the patient is to have any hope of getting better. Once out of the operating room, Mac Tools' focus shifted from survival to once again becoming a great company.

John Aden measured the company's improvement in terms much broader and, ultimately, more important than financial results alone. Actions they took resulted in changed lives! "The clearest indicator came from being with people, having real interactions and feeling part of their hearts. I saw that by pouring ourselves into people, good things were able to happen." In an employee survey, taken across all the parent company divisions, results confirmed a remarkable turnaround. Data covering job satisfaction, work environment, morale and so on, placed Mac Tools' people at or near the top of all the Stanley Works divisions—quite amazing in light of the convulsive changes.

KEYS TO A CHANGED COMPANY

While the kind of radical turnaround experienced by Mac Tools involved thousands of actions, three steps had the greatest impact as the company built toward the future. The first was to get the management team aligned around a common vision. John took the initiative: "I felt we were on the verge of something great, because I learned early that from big breakdowns come big breakthroughs."

To see this breakthrough happen, John engaged the company's leadership in a process to decide between three possible directions: being *customer intimate*, focusing on *product excellence* or establishing *operational excellence*. (Michael Treacy and Fred Wiersema develop these alternate "value disciplines" in detail in their book on business strategy, *The Discipline of Market Leaders*.)

Ultimately the management team agreed their primary focus should be customer intimacy—to provide their customers superior solutions all the time, whether in their product, services or support. (In essence, Mac Tools was really defining its purpose—the priority we discussed in chapter eight.) If successful, their new focus would produce "customers for life"—a theme that became widely publicized inside the company and beyond. "Those on our leadership team became passionate about bringing our vision to life." With a clear focus, they began developing initiatives, actions they could take behind the scenes to affirm the course they were taking.

The second step came out of a need that surfaced from this first action. As they met together, it became evident that key leaders were more concerned about "being right" than thinking through what was best for the company—a mindset that fueled unneeded conflict among the leadership. Consequently the management team decided they would establish a set of guidelines governing acceptable and unacceptable behavior during meetings and other interactions. From these came expectations they implemented company-wide in the form of six operating values:

- Each of us is 100 percent **Responsible**.

- We treat others with **Respect**.

- We honor each other's **Contributions.**

- We are **Aligned** and operate as **One Team.**

- We operate with **Unquestionable Integrity.**

- We foster an environment for **Continuous Learning.**

From the outset, leaders were expected to confront behavior that was inconsistent with the company's values. Aden told them, "Your commitment to these values will be tested." Tested they were, and within a short time, two of his direct reports had to be replaced. Clear values in the interactive process led to a "pruning" of the leadership to a team of people who fully bought in.

The first two principal ways John Aden *served* his company—by helping it clarify its *vision* and by establishing clear operating *values*—produced undeniable improvement. The third step was more subtle, but equally critical. It was to *communicate*, deeply and broadly, the principles that were most important to the company, especially their vision and values. Significantly, John realized his effectiveness would hinge on who he was as a person, and a "new" John Aden was being forged in the midst of his company's transformation.

CHANGING LIVES

John was becoming increasingly aware of how his growing faith in Christ intersected his work, and specifically how Jesus could guide him in his leadership role. "Looking at Jesus' approach to leadership sparked some radical changes in me," John said. "For example, Jesus led by walking around, telling stories and being with people. That phrase 'being with people' meant Jesus wasn't keeping them at arm's length. He wasn't simply 'tolerating' them, only pretending to listen. He really was *with* them."

For John this was a huge adjustment. "I had been promoted very rapidly in my former jobs. At age 30 I was running a division of Frito-Lay with $400 million in sales and 2,000 people. I thought I had it all figured out. But with what I've learned in this process, even the things I did here in the first two years would be done with a different motivation." Then John added, "So here I am, after these two years, and God is changing *my* life!" This became obvious to more than 2,500 of Mac Tools' customers at a recent company event.

A DIFFERENT COMPANY GATHERING

John says, "Normally, we'd begin our annual meeting with a big 'hurrah.' We'd have a dramatic video build up, and I'd ride on stage on a Harley. It was all about *me!* But this time I sat in the audience with a microphone—not on stage at all. I said, 'What I have to tell you today is so important that I can't let this meeting be about me—the Harley and all. It's got to be about you guys.' Then we presented a video that honored the spouses of our Mac Tool people. We had never done that before."

But John had more to say, so toward the close of the meeting he went on stage. He knew there was a hard-core group in the audience who would be cynical about what he was about to do, but that didn't deter him. They weren't the people he was trying to reach. "I pointed to a number of stuffed burlap bags, commenting that these represented the 'stories' we have in our lives. They make us who we are. For example, we learned on the school playground that we shouldn't cry. Later we heard a disgruntled uncle say he hated his job, and that became our view of work."

By now the audience had become very quiet. John continued: "These stories can be positive or negative, but they determine who we are. Now here's the problem. Negative stories can hold us back, keeping us from realizing our full potential." Then John became very personal. "I grabbed some sacks of my own, threw each over my shoulder. Here's one that says 'I'm a pretty good guy on my own—came to Mac Tool this way.' Here's another one. It's got stuff I heard from great leaders, like when you're the boss, you need to always be right—don't ever let your people see you be wrong. Then here's another sack. It says you can't have friends in the workplace. And another—it says that values I have at home and who I am can't come into the workplace. I even have stories in my life that say, 'I come to work every day so you guys can serve me.'"

Then John threw all the sacks down in a big pile and said, "I want to put these behind me. I always want to be informed by these stories, but I'm committed to taking power away from them. I don't want to be a guy who can't develop real relationships in the workplace. I don't want to be a guy who can't bring my personal values to work every day. I don't want to come to work ever again saying, 'You're here for me.' I really want to learn to serve you. I'm committed to being a different kind of leader. I'm going to live out my life in front of everybody."

John told me that as a result of his comments, "something changed in this company forever." After the meeting he walked the hallway, and people came up in tears saying, "There are things I've been carrying for decades. Now I know I can put those things behind me."

IT BEGINS WITH THE LEADER

When I began my interview with John Aden for this chapter of *Mastering Monday*, I had no idea how much he would let me see into his own heart as a leader. I was so impressed with the deep transformation underway in his life and how it is affecting the way he's running his company. John may not favor the term "servant leader," as noted earlier, but from my observation, he is indeed a leader who is serving the Lord and serving his company in some groundbreaking and significant ways. His final insights, which follow, could be a model for everyone who seeks to lead and influence others—especially the importance of personal transparency.

> One of the most valuable lessons I'm learning is how important transparency is. Life isn't perfect. When I come to work indicating that everything is perfect, what I really do is screw up the people around me who are going home every day saying, "I wish I had what Aden does because my life is kind of rotten right now." The truth is we're all struggling. As leaders we have an obligation to live out some of our messy moments, and for me, that's to be frank about who I was before as a leader. This is where real learning takes place. We serve by allowing ourselves to be "imperfect people," and for that to be OK. I now realize being transparent is tremendously freeing, especially closing the gap between who I am at home and who I am in the workplace.

RELIGION IN THE WORKPLACE

With great determination, John is working through the visible merging of what he believes as a Christian and the "secular" atmosphere of the work world. "There are all kinds of lies people live by, such as the prohibition against bringing religion into the workplace. I've come to see it isn't a religion problem, but a communication problem. I can go out and ride my Harley with other people, or work out at the gym with fellow employees. But if I pray with people, for some this is over the top. Everything 'hits the fan.' However, because I'm willing to 'live my life out loud' in every area, I get greater latitude when it comes to the spiritual side of my life."

Some independent feedback to John is reassuring. "Consultants have told me in the past, 'You'll get fired for bringing your faith into the workplace.' Now they're saying, 'Because you've made your life so transparent, it's not an issue anymore.' So now we have a group of people from the company that meets after hours twice each month, and I attend with all the others—and whoever's there, we just pray."

A LEADER'S HEART

As he is with the people in his company, John Aden was transparent with me. "I want to say that God is really working inside, in my heart. For the past two years, I've been asking God to help me really love people. That's a change for me from who I was. It's to imagine people experiencing life and purpose in a way that far exceeds anything I could ever dream for them. The leader I want to be is the person who really loves and cares for my people. It means getting my pride out of the way, and to really encourage and serve the people around me."

I asked John if he found the concept of service to be in conflict with other corporate objectives. "That's a challenging question," he said.

There may seem to be times when our concept of service is in conflict with other goals, such as meeting our financial targets. Sometimes my emotional drawer is full from the great things that are happening with people, but my financial drawer isn't. Pride comes up a lot, especially when our team is focused solely on "hitting the numbers." Ego *and* paychecks are involved. But I'd rather focus on our mission, not to the exclusion of our financial goals but recognizing they are just part of the whole. I'm confident we're making human investments that will produce tremendous results some day. We do it because it's the right thing, not because it always flows through to the bottom line.

The numbers are only one measure of assessing what we're really up to in life. Most important are our people. We want to create careers for our people that are significant—more than just a job—and in this way communicate our genuine care for them. People have a strong desire to achieve and be respected, but they often think they *achieve* at work and are *significant* at home. I'm trying to create a culture where these lines between achievement and significance are not parallel, but actually cross.

John concluded not by shifting responsibility to others but by placing it on himself:

I understand that I have to take the lead. What I'm talking about, like corporate values or ethical behavior, is not something I can delegate to the HR department. I can't say, "Go put together a values program and we'll roll it out to the company." Our whole conversation is not about a program. It's not about technique. It's about a leader's heart change. And it takes a lot of work for a person to have a change of heart. It starts with me. And it takes consistently living out what I believe. Having a servant's heart, having values, can't jump a whole level of the organization. It must be consistent from the top down. The whole organization feels it when there's inconsistency in a leader's values. The motives have to be right."

Though John didn't say it specifically, it's clear that perseverance has been essential in his service to Mac Tools. Getting the company to its current stage of transformation has been a wearing, grinding process. But John has taken a long-term view so characteristic of great leaders. His bold, shorter-range actions have been essential ingredients of a large plan. And the centerpiece of his successful efforts has been his wholehearted commitment to serve.

BUSINESS: A TEMPLATE FOR SERVICE

In 1990 Lawrence M. Miller wrote a book called *Barbarians to Bureaucrats: Corporate Life Cycle Strategies*. In it he said that businesses develop along similar paths, beginning entrepreneurially and moving into a rapid growth phase. Then they typically level off at the midpoint of a bell-shaped curve. At that point in the growth cycle businesses can become flawed in two critical ways: becoming bureaucratic and looking inward. To avoid sliding down the second half of the bell-curve (sometimes to oblivion), two countermeasures are necessary: bust bureaucracy and focus outward, passionately serving customers.

Focusing on those who buy our products or services is a strong prescription for an organization's health. It was essential for Mac Tools. They reshaped their entire organization around building "customers for life," fueled by John Aden's realization that they had lost touch with their customer base.

What applies in recovering from a crisis can apply just as well before the crisis hits. Every enterprise that hopes to succeed *must* have a compelling and comprehensive drive to serve their customers with distinction. Here are some excerpts from language we use in our own company. We pledge to

- be close to our customers at all levels and include them in activities that drive optimum solutions.

- be very easy to do business with.

- be fanatical about listening, being responsive and following through on commitments, while avoiding any kind of arrogance or indifference.

When such a perspective becomes normative in a business, people throughout become servants, ultimately focusing outward on the customer. The customer becomes the locomotive that pulls the rest of the train, getting all the railcars moving in the same direction. People learn to serve each other internally, because that's the only way to support the external mission. Put another way, a focus outward results in a serving-oriented organization throughout.

Our company was recently on the receiving end of such service with a new supplier. We had made a firm commitment to provide a molded plastic component to one of our largest customers as part of their new product launch. Our supplier for the component had received raw plastic material they couldn't work with, but we didn't know their dilemma until Friday. We were due to ship to our customer early the following week. Several of our people had sleepless nights over the weekend. Would this unproven supplier come through, and could we weather the black eye we would receive with our customer if they let us down? Well, come through they did, their production people working double shifts over the weekend. Guaranteed—that supplier has catapulted up the list of companies we want to do business with the next time.

Business can become a powerful engine for serving, internally and to the outside customer. This is exactly how Mac Tools has reshaped its culture. It began with John Aden as the president, but is now working throughout the entire organization. At our company, we likewise spell out the role of leadership in this process:

> A chief function of management is to *serve* subordinates—to set clear goals, encourage initiative, give positive reinforcement, remove roadblocks, secure needed resources (including help from others) and evaluate and recognize progress.

How does this apply where you work? Are you focusing on service as a priority? Is your work customer driven? What about serving internal clients—your fellow workers? My conclusion, and John Aden is a great example, is that a follower of Christ who embraces the theme of service can be a tremendous influence in his or her organization and a catalyst to organizational health. Jesus is the model, for he was the greatest servant of all. And he deeply wants to implant his heart and spirit of service in each of us.

■ ■ ■

As we near the close of *Mastering Monday*, take a moment to think back over this section's five themes: Purpose, Values, People, Stewardship and Service. I've found they become more firmly anchored in my mind and heart as I knit them together in this prayer:

Lord, I ask for clarity of Purpose in my life and in my work. Help me to always be rooted in enduring Core Values, to see People as you see them and value them deeply. Might I regard all that I have as yours, on loan to wisely Steward. And might I Serve you and others with all my heart.

Epilogue

I believe one of the next great moves of God

is going to be through the believers in the workplace.

BILLY GRAHAM

That your ways may be known on earth,

your salvation among all nations.

PSALM 67:2

We began our journey in this book's preface with the notion that Monday—that often-maligned first day of the workweek—could be mastered. As we conclude that journey, I'm sure you have noted that it is really the Master himself who enables us to master our work, to "Master Monday."

In our journey to master Monday, we met some biblical role models like Noah, Moses, David and Daniel, as well as modern-day business leaders—people like David Pugh, Archie Dunham, Anne Beiler and John Aden. These examples are inspiring companions on the journey, encouraging us that God has his hand on everyday saints. They are not so different from you and me. Quietly, steadily, they are bringing a kingdom perspective to circles of influence that are strategically important to God's ultimate purposes. If only more people of their character and effectiveness occupied executive suites across the land. Unfortunately, they don't.

SCANDALS AND SERVANTS

Recently a top executive with one of the world's largest companies was cited for improper use of his corporate expense account. Estimates of his alleged fraud range from $100,000 to $500,000. Though this is far from "small change," it is extraordinary that he might have engaged in such practices in light of his $6 million annual income from the company. I spoke with one of his former associates who was incredulous. "It's crazy," he said. "I worked closely with him for over two decades and thought I knew him. I haven't the slightest idea why he might have done this." Sadly this is but one of many scandals over the past few years involving prominent corporate leaders, several of whom are currently awaiting sentencing or are already in prison. Collectively these abuses have given corporate America its largest black eye ever.

But there's another story currently being written: the transforming effect more and more of God's servants are having on their businesses. I recently spent a day with one group in particular, the CEO Forum, which has some 150 members. All are heading up large businesses, including several Fortune 500 companies. Amazingly, the combined employment of these businesses exceeds five million people. These men and women aren't pursuing "business as usual." Rather, they are allowing the Lord to work powerfully in their lives as they grow to become spiritual statesmen. Their work in the companies they lead is quiet, but highly effective. And none are making headlines for corrupt workplace activities.

The CEO Forum is but one of several outstanding organizations worldwide whose members are seeking to advance God's kingdom in the marketplace. I've gotten to know other groups up close, including the Christian Businessman's Committee (CBMC), with some 18,000 members in the United States; the Full Gospel Business Men's Fellowship International (FGBMFI), active in over 130 countries; the Fellowship of Companies for Christ (FCCI) and the International Christian Chamber of Commerce (ICCC). I've been deeply impressed as I've met with local and regional marketplace ministries, from Boston to San Jose, from Calgary to Houston.

A WORLDWIDE MOVEMENT

I've seen firsthand the far-flung dimensions of this movement in such unlikely places as Hungary, Israel, the former Soviet Union and Ecuador. Indeed throughout the world there is growing momentum for believers to live godly lives and carry their high personal standards into their work. Recently I was able to participate in inaugural introductions of the work-faith movement into the North African nation of Morocco and into mainland China. Even in these countries that are "closed" to the gospel, I've found it possible to bring a faith perspective regarding work.

Os Hillman, in his book *Faith@Work,* substantiates rapid growth in the work-faith movement:

> In the last twelve years there is a new paradigm in workplace ministry unfolding. Twelve years ago we could identify only 25 formalized workplace ministries. Today, we have identi-

fied 1,200 organizations that seek to integrate faith and work. These include non-profit workplace ministries, educational institutions, business organizations and churches that intentionally focus on faith and work. This incredible rate of growth is why many are saying that there is a genuine move of God taking place in this arena that has the potential for changing the spiritual landscape in the local church and cities and nations.

Meanwhile, major media have taken note, with cover stories and major articles appearing in *Fortune* magazine, *Business Week*, *Industry Week*, *The New York Times*, *The Wall Street Journal* and many other media outlets. Virtually every major TV network has done feature stories on this modern phenomenon.

Events of September 11, 2001, in New York City, Washington, D.C., and farmlands in western Pennsylvania provided added impetus to the movement, emboldening corporate leaders to be more visible in proclaiming their deepest convictions. One, Steve Reinemund, the CEO of PepsiCo, gave opportunity on that fateful day for employees to join in prayer at the company's headquarters just outside New York City. Remarkably, nearly all twelve hundred employees participated. Matt Rose, CEO of Burlington Northern Santa Fe Railroad, had a similar experience at BNSF's headquarters in Fort Worth, Texas.

STEWARDING GOD'S FOCUS ON THE WORKPLACE

By any measure, there is tremendous momentum for faith and work to converge. Small streams flowing across the business landscape just a decade ago have become large rivers. God's kingdom is breaking through into the marketplace in authentic and unprecedented ways.

The history of spiritual movements reminds us we must not take this move of God for granted. Though we may not understand all the reasons for God's current focus, it is vital that we acknowledge his activity and fully cooperate with the opportunities presented. How often in other such powerful waves of spiritual activity have we have seen their impact squandered through neglect—their cutting edge permanently lost?

The words of General Douglas MacArthur, while applying to warfare, echo a warning well suited to our current challenge in business:

> The history of failure in war can be summed up in two words: *Too late.* Too late in realizing the danger, too late in preparedness, too late in uniting all possible force for resistance, too late in standing with our friends.

There is indeed an urgency to seize the moment, to not be too late, to embrace God's far-reaching activity in the marketplace and join him in what he is initiating and achieving.

CALLED, COMMISSIONED, SENT

Jesus' words at the close of his time on earth should erase any doubt in our minds. He clearly wants each of us "out there," going into "all the world" to engage in a high-risk, high-reward lifestyle to extend his kingdom on earth. He is calling and commissioning us not to retreat to safe havens but to permeate and transform every sphere into which he sends us—clothed not in our own strength but in his. "My prayer is not that you take them out of the world but that you protect them from the evil one" (John 17:15). Our mission parallels his own: "As You [Father] sent Me into the world, I also have sent them into the world" (John 17:18 NKJV).

This aggressive posture doesn't square with many in today's church who are convinced the only way to avoid being *of* the world is to avoid being *in* the world. Risks run rampant, to be sure, that by our venturing *into* the world, we'll be ensnared *by* the world. But such a view has allowed multitudes of believers to remain disengaged, large segments of society to be abandoned and evil to advance unchecked.

Billy Graham offers a keen insight on this ever-present challenge to be engaged in the world without being overwhelmed and nullified by its influence. Likening our role in the world to that of the Gulf Stream in the ocean, he observes:

> The Gulf Stream is in the ocean, and yet it is not a part of it. Believers are in the world, and yet they must not be absorbed by it. The Gulf Stream maintains its warm temperatures even in the icy water of the North Atlantic. If Christians are to fulfill their purposes in the world, they must not be chilled by the indifferent, godless society in which they live. (*Decision* magazine, February 2005)

Do you know that palm trees grow on islands off the west coast of Scotland? Yet Siberia, which endures some of the world's harshest winters, is on a similar latitude—just farther east. The difference is the Gulf Stream. Does it excite you, as it does me, to know we've been called, commissioned and sent *into* a world that is unredeemed, full of darkness and even hostile to those who believe?

Does it challenge you to refuse to be assimilated, to retain a distinct, climate-changing identity? Are you destined to be a warm and welcome Gulf Stream in the chilly Atlantic?

As I cited earlier:

God is continually preparing his heroes, and when the opportunity is right, he puts them into position in an instant. He works so fast, the world wonders where they came from.

I encourage you to be one of God's heroes—a spiritual leader who has learned to Master Monday.

May you burn with a passion to make a difference. May you brilliantly radiate the light of Christ. Right where you are. Right in the workplace. Every Monday morning!

About the Author

John D. Beckett was born and grew up in Elyria, Ohio, the oldest of three children. After attending public schools in Elyria, he graduated from M.I.T. in 1960 with a bachelor of science in economics and mechanical engineering. Following graduation he worked as an engineer in the aerospace industry.

He joined his father in a small family-owned manufacturing business in 1963, becoming president in 1965 upon the death of his father. He is now chairman of the company and has helped guide the business to worldwide leadership in the manufacture and sale of engineered components for residential and commercial heating. The company, with its affiliates, currently has sales exceeding $100 million, with over 600 employees.

Mr. Beckett has long been active in both church and community-related activities. He helped found Intercessors For America, a national prayer organization, in 1973 and continues to serve as its board chairman. He is a founding board member of The King's College in New York City, a director of Graphic Packaging Corporation, a NYSE-listed manufacturing company, and serves on the board of Campus Crusade for Christ, International.

His first book, *Loving Monday: Succeeding in Business Without*

Selling Your Soul, was published in 1998 by InterVarsity Press. The book is Mr. Beckett's account of how he has sought to practically integrate his faith and his work. It is currently available in twelve international editions. In 1999 the Christian Broadcasting Network named him "Christian Businessman of the Year." Mr. Beckett received an honorary Doctor of Laws degree from Spring Arbor University in 2002, and was named manufacturing "Entrepreneur of the Year" by Ernst & Young in 2003.

Mr. Beckett resides in Elyria, Ohio, with his wife, Wendy, to whom he has been married since 1961. They are the parents of six children and grandparents of eleven.

www.masteringmonday.com
www.lovingmonday.com
www.beckettcorp.com
www.lifesgreatestquestion.com